The Fermanagh Miscellany 2011

Edited by Dianne Trimble and John Cunningham

Fermanagh Authors' Association
Enniskillen 2011

COPYRIGHT NOTICE

No part of this book may be reproduced or may be transmitted in any form or by means electronic or mechanical, including photocopy, recording or any information storage or retrieval system without permission in writing from the author.

© Individual authors
© Concept copyright Fermanagh Authors' Association

ISBN – 978-1-907530-20-3

The Janus Figure in Caldragh Graveyard, Boa Island, Co. Fermanagh is one of the central images in the poetry of Francis Harvey and the title of one of his collections of poetry, The Boa Island Janus (1996). Dating back to pre-Christian Ireland this statue with two faces expresses the duality of his upbringing with a Presbyterian father and a Catholic mother a theme which he frequently returned to.

Contents

Preface	3
Dedication	4
Talking To A Ghost Bryan Gallagher	6
Fermanagh's Little Piece Of Heaven And Reflections For An Anniversary Mass Fr Brian D'Arcy	8
Too Much Tannin Winston Graydon	11
Fermanagh's Teenage Writing Sensation In 1927 – Myrtle Johnston John Cunningham	14
Poems: *Unbound, Repair, 3 Letterboy Road* Mary Montague	23
The Dinner Girl John Reihill	25
The Lammasman, born August First 1930 Sean McElgunn	30
Heritage On The High Street Dianne Trimble	31
Roslea Wedding 1819	35
Pictures Of The Past Sean McElgunn	39
When London Trees Let Down Their Leaves Tony Brady	41
Poems: *Autumn Revelation, An Haiku, The End Of An Era* Tony Brady	42
The Funeral Of Jemmy Leonard Frank McHugh	44
The Drainage On The Upper Erne John Foynes	45
Some Reflections On The Erne Hydroelectricity Scheme Michael Donnelly	46
Wellington, The Iron Duke And A Bit Of An Enigma Vicky Herbert	53

And Now Let's Hear It For The Duck John Cunningham	58
Poems: *Never Finish, Ode To The Scots 17-03-09* Ruthanne Baxter	63
Poolside Red Alert Ruthanne Baxter	65
A Link To Her Past Dianne Trimble	67
Cahir McKeown's Early Memories	72
Watching For A Drink Sean McElgunn	76
Poems: *The Sun Shone, With Thanks* Julie Richmond	78
Moorehead's Gander Winston Graydon	80
The South-Fermanagh Almanack And Directory 1896 Dermot Maguire	82
Directories	86
Obituaries: *Rose McCaughey, Johnny McKeagney*	97
T P Flanagan Remembered Michael Donnelly	99
T P Flanagan Remembered Dermot Maguire	101
Ar Ais Go Keriolet – Back To Keriolet Reviewed Michael Donnelly	102
Fermanagh Publications 2010	104
Contributors	105

Preface

The publication of our fifth annual *Fermanagh Miscellany* is another notable achievement in the life of the Fermanagh Authors' Association. The production of five annual journals in succession without financial assistance is no mean achievement in what is a very challenging world for books in general. The advent of eBooks of all kinds and the difficulty of finding outlets is making life difficult for all authors especially those depending on local sales. Traditional bookshops are closing down due to fierce competition from the Internet and the large supermarket chains and secondhand bookshops are closing as a result of competition from Charity Shops who get their books for free. We welcome some new contributors and writers this year as well as those who have appeared in our journals before. We have an increase in poetry and creative writing in this issue while historical and reminiscence items are well to the fore as usual. Our writers have had their work appear in many journals and newspapers during the year and Seamas Mac Annaidh records the publications of the past year by Fermanagh writers, many of whom are members of Fermanagh Authors' Association.

Dianne Trimble and John Cunningham (Joint Editors)

As a step towards the future this book has also been produced as an eBook. We sincerely hope that books will never disappear but we have to recognise present trends in publishing.

IDENTITIES

Fermanagh: half in and half out
of whatever its element is,
never quite sure at any time

whether it's one thing or the other,
land in water or water in land,
but amphibious like me amid

the fluencies and insularities that
lie even deeper than land or water and
host here in this graveyard by the lake

among the tussocked and hummocked graves
of Boa Island's Christian dead
to a squat twin-headed stone idol

that was looking two ways long before
I knew there were two ways of looking
upstream to a source and downstream to the sea.

Francis Harvey.

Dedication

Francis Harvey

This year's *Fermanagh Miscellany* is dedicated to Francis Harvey. Known primarily as a poet Francis Harvey, who was born in Enniskillen in 1925, is Fermanagh's senior literary figure. His *Collected Poems,* which contains work from his four previous collections as well as many new poems, was published in 2007 to considerable acclaim. He has also written radio plays and short stories. Last year he was elected a member of Aos Dána, the assembly of Ireland's most significant arts practitioners.

Harvey is also significant from a local history perspective as his parents came from two notable local families, his father Hamilton Harvey was a son of James Harvey the contractor who built many of the most important buildings in Enniskillen including the townhall and the Presbyterian church. His mother Anne Cassidy belonged to a prominent Ballyshannon family. And so he writes, in his poem 'Mixed Marriage' –

> Fare thee well, Inniskilling!
> Fare thee well, Inis Ceithleann!
> I come of bridge-builders whose
> Stones, plumb, spanned more than water.

His 1996 collection, *The Boa Island Janus,* explores this background which he defines as upstream (Enniskillen) and downstream (Ballyshannon). The Janus is the stone idol that looks in two directions and the young Harvey gradually realised that he had two traditions he could draw from. He writes of watching the 12th of July parades from his Belmore Street window with his mother –

> Even then
> as we peered out at them through the lace-curtain mists
> of our sitting-room window, uneasy
> as wood kernes, I was learning to keep
> my distance and learning history too
> as I watched you breaking cover and showing
> yourself at the window as they withdrew.

In 'Foray' he gives us glimpses of himself and the other boys from St. Michael's Intermediate School going up to Portora 'fearful of ambush' to sit state examinations.

In 'Icons' he tells of how his mother had put up a cardboard print of Jesus in their house but it was only later on that he realised that his father would have thought this peculiar.

> the cobwebbed Christ I was too young to
> understand my father must have thought such
> a strange thing there. As strange as those pictures
> of the King and Queen I used to see
> in the houses of his people were to me.

Another potent symbol is the poppy. In 'The Language of Flowers' he writes:

> In Belmore Street I wore my poppy for
> The dead in war, for my father too and
> His forebears and for my mother's mother
> Who came from that same stock. I wear it now
> In memory of the Enniskillen dead,
> The wounds they wore that day like poppies bled.

In one of the most moving poems in the collection he writes about going to visit the zoo with his parents at a time when his father was dying from cancer but as a child being only vaguely aware that all was not as it should be.

> a world I'd
> sometimes glimpsed when for no reason at all
> grown-ups would suddenly burst into tears
> or kiss or, like my parents now, constantly
> reach out to touch each other and touch me.

Similarly it is only years later that he realises that the Presentation Brother who taught him at school suffered from terrible loneliness

> trapped in
> the limbo he taught us was close to hell.

Another figure from his childhood to feature in the collection is Enniskillen wheelwright James Orr whom he thought of

> as Joseph
> the Worker ankle-deep in shavings
> of oak and ash with his array of tools
>
> spokeshaves, awls,
> planes, gouges, chisels, saws, all those names for
> the mystery of love and how it works
> even when its working against the grain.

In other collections, although Harvey does refer sometimes to his Enniskillen childhood, much of the focus moves to Donegal where he has lived for many years. He celebrates the harsh and beautiful landscapes where he loves to walk and he shows a great compassion for the people who had to eke out a livelihood in such an unforgiving terrain. As Moya Cannon states in her introduction to *Collected Poems*

> The rendered beauty of the landscapes which he sees with a painter's eye is all the more convincing because he does not flinch from the harshness of the granite landscapes or from the material poverty of the lives lived by the sheep farmers who cling to them.

Francis Harvey has created a considerable body of work and is still writing at 86. We celebrate his achievement and wish him well.

Talking To A Ghost

by Bryan Gallagher

My uncle was 53 when he and his young family emigrated to New York from a hungry mountainside in North Leitrim. He had left it too late.

They said that at the foot of the aeroplane steps he stopped and made an attempt to go back.

Along with the good navy blue suit, the shirt with detachable collars, the box of collar studs and the pair of light boots, he had packed his fiddle and his bow, lovingly wrapped in sheets of newspaper. But he never played it in America and it stayed in a bottom drawer in yellowing sheets of *The Leitrim Observer*.

His letters were all about home with never a mention of his new life, and always, always he wanted to know what was the price of black cattle in Collooney Fair.

On the one occasion he came back, he made his way to the house where my father and he were reared and with a pliers he pulled from the kitchen wall, the nail on which we used to hang his fiddle. He brought it back to his New York home, hammered it into the wall there and that night, he played 'The Boys of Ballisodare' and hung his fiddle on it again. I went back to North Leitrim some years ago to visit the old house. I had been there once before as a child with my father. Now I carried my own son on my shoulders.

Round a bend up a steep lane I suddenly came face to face with an old man coming down. He stopped and looked at me and said 'Eddie'.

"That was my father's name," I said.

Well if your father was made young again, that's him walking up the lane. He spoke in that courtly way you only find in country places, and he turned round to walk back a bit with me and show me the way. He kept looking at me as if he couldn't believe his eyes.

"Would there be any chance that you would come back and do up the house," he said. "I would love to see someone above me on the mountain".

"There was smoke from all those chimneys," he said, pointing out the ruined houses on the mountain face. "I rambled in every one of those houses, but they're all gone now."

"Did you never think of going away yourself," I asked.

"I never was further than Collooney fair," he said. "Never further than the fair of Collooney."

"What about your family," I said.

"I have a son in Philadelphia," he said. "I was out to see him last year. I have another son in Los Angeles. I went out to him the year before. It's on the far side of America. The lane's bad but it's dry underfoot. Mind the little fellow."

Gentle regular undulations of the grass were all that marked where my uncle's garden of brown sharp-edged ridges had been. Nettles and brambles were growing up to the open doorway. The boy wrinkled his nose at the smell of the calves in the kitchen. And through the broken window I could still see the nail hole in the wall and the tracks of his pliers in the flaking pink distemper.

When I had seen enough I turned to go.

The old man was waiting for me at a gap in the hedge. He had a paper bag in his hands. "There's some apples for the boy. My two lads always liked them. You were always a fine big man, Eddie," and he was gone through the gap in the hedge.

I didn't know if he was sane or mad. It was a strange and unsettling conversation.

In the car when I opened the bag, the apples had hard cracked skin and black spots from years of neglect, but the flesh inside was sweet and wholesome. And as I looked at them I realised that the old man had not spoken to me at all. He had been talking to a ghost, the ghost of a long-dead neighbour that he had met walking up a lane in Leitrim.

Fermanagh's Little Piece of Heaven and Reflections for an Anniversary Mass

by Fr Brian D'Arcy

Fermanagh is a little piece of heaven to me. I became even more aware of our beautiful county when I was asked to offer Mass for a life-long friend Gerry Ryan. It was a bitter disappointment when Gerry's drug taking became a major talking point after his untimely death. His family were subjected to huge media pressures and his sudden death left many unanswered questions. For his fans, his friends, his work colleagues, and most of all for Morah and the children, the year ended, as it began, in sadness and division.

When Morah, his wife, asked me to offer Mass for Gerry's family and close friends on the first Anniversary, I needed words of comfort or hope, but none came easily.

On the night before the Mass, friends suggested that Inish Davar would be worth a visit. It was the end of April and the bluebells were in bloom and might not last much longer. Against my better judgement I went to the island.

We arrived on the boat and I couldn't wait to see the island of about 20 acres completely carpeted in bluebells. Yet as I walked onto the island it was not the bluebells but the blossoms on the trees which drew me in. The trees were beautiful. Most of them were thorn trees and the pink and white blossoms stood out against the setting sun on a breezy, balmy evening.

As I stood and watched the trees I became aware of one special tree that was leafless and naked. The last time I was on the island that particular tree was perfectly dressed in full foliage. I remember listening to a little bird with a wonderful singing voice standing on the top branch making marvellous music from the hidden recesses of the layers of leaves.

This evening though, the tree was a lifeless skeleton obviously killed by the winter frost. Still the little bird came back to sing his song of triumph from the very top of the now dead tree.

The other trees were mad alive, but the little bird singing on top of the dead tree told me that God uses even dead things to affirm life. It was a haunting life-giving moment.

I moved on to admire the bluebells. I sauntered through the paths. There was a magic carpet of bluebells over the entire island. The only places with no bluebells were the paths which people and animals made to move through the island.

I noticed that there were a few albino or white bluebells. One of them stood out. It was a bluebell in every respect except colour. It had its own unique beauty. It told me we can be different and still be beautiful; different but still part of the team.

There were other white flowers, perhaps even weeds, pushing up through the bluebells. A few days later the bluebells will still be there, but won't be noticeable because the white weeds will smother them. But this evening it was just perfect, a tinge of white under a carpet of blue.

As the light faded I made my way to the water's edge to watch the setting sun. It wasn't a blood red sun. It was a genuinely sun-coloured sun. It was a perfect sphere dropping gently out of the sky and resting on Lough Erne. We stood at the water's edge for 20 minutes in silence as the sun rested on the calm waters of Lough Erne and then in a matter of minutes the sun went to sleep in its watery bed.

We knew it was a rare, precious moment and in time we talked about it. Life goes on. Thousands of years before Christ, that very same sun sank in that very same place and apart from changed vegetation on the island, not much else was different a few thousand years later.

As we walked back through the bluebells the darker light allowed them to show off their pure colour. When the sun went to bed the bluebells took on a fluorescent hue.

When I came home I went into our little chapel in The Graan and thought about God's creation. Nature teaches us that God's creation has no problem with death because it always results in new life. Now I had a story for Gerry Ryan's Mass.

We humans are part of the transient creatures of this earth. The trees that I admired gave hope to other human beings fifty, sixty maybe a hundred years ago. They will probably do the same for people 50 years from now when I'll be dead and gone.

When I went to offer Mass for Gerry Ryan the next morning, I began by telling Morah, the children and the friends present that it had been a tough and sad and awful year for them. But they have survived the first birthday, the first Christmas, the first Easter and now the first anniversary. At one time they were too frightened to even think about a future. But because they worked together, encouraged and listened to each other, they survived. I then told them the story of the island, the bird, the dead tree, the beautifully groomed trees, the bluebells, the weeds and the setting sun. The images proved life-giving and comforting to them too.

Afterwards in Gerry's house, Gerry's friends remembered only the story of the island. Bono (of U2 fame) and his wife Ali were fascinated by the singing bird on the dead tree. We talked for an hour about finding hope in the reality of life and death.

As I left for home Bono joked: "When you write another Volume of your Memoirs you have the perfect title for it. Call it, 'The Tree Was Dead, But The Bird Still Sang.'

When I arrived home I prayed. The images became a metaphor for my own efforts at life. Why do we continue to look for the living among the dead? I don't know but the bird's song was hauntingly life-giving even though his pulpit was a dead tree.

At Sunday Mass I told them again about our Bluebell island. One of those listening was a 6 year old child. She went home, and unknown to her parents she drew a straight line of perfect bluebells on a white sheet of paper. Then she drew an orange sun setting behind them. To the left was a match-stick man (me I presume). To the right was a tree with a bird singing on a branch. The tree was covered in green foliage. When her mother asked her why, the 6 year old replied: "I just couldn't bring myself to draw a dead tree."

Out of the mouths of babes…..

Too Much Tannin
by Winston Graydon

Sandy Gray and Paddy Finn, who were neighbours for many years, were talking about the old times and how things had changed and how the custom of going on your kailey was dying out altogether.

'Ah sure Sandy,' said Paddy, 'people haven't time for the like a that nowadays. Long ago people had no transport except maybe an oul bicycle and nothin' else to do on the long winter nights. Goin' on your kailey was the only bit a entertainment they had and anyway no-one would want ye sittin' half the night takin' up their time an keepin' them out a bed. It's a thing a the past.'

'Paddy, did I ever tell ye about a man called Willie Smith? He was a great man for goin' on his kailey. You might say he was a professional at it. He went from one house to another on a regular basis and was always lookin' for tay and wouldn't leave 'til he got it, should it be one or two o'clock in the morning. Of course Paddy as you know it was always the custom to give visitors a drop a tay before they left but Willie always overdid it.'

'Did he overstay his welcome, Sandy?' asked Paddy wittingly.

'Ah sure the neighbours were sick of him, Paddy, couldn't get rid a him, and de ye know this? If Willie thought the woman a the house was a bit long in gettin' round to wettin' the tay, he was rale bare faced about droppin' hints like, 'Boys that kettle's fairly boilin now' or 'Me throat's very dry the night' or 'It'll not be long til I will have to be goin' even though he had no intention a goin' til the tay was made but tryin' to encourage the woman a the house to say, 'You'll take a sup a tay in your hand before ye go. And of course the people that Willie happened to kailey with would be droppin' hints to try and get him to go. Things like startin' to rake the fire or puttin' the cat out or even startin' to take their boots off.'

'Boys Sandy, you would a felt like takin' the poker to a man like that!' said Paddy.

'Ah sure Paddy, I suppose many a one felt like doin' it but he never shifted til he got the tay and a couple a pieces a fadge bread and usually sayin' 'I'm runnin' now when I get the tay.' Anyway to come to the best part a the story Paddy, a couple a smart boys that made their kailey from time to time in a house that Willie was in the same night struck on a rale good plan to put the tay out a Willie's head and of course everyone in the house that night were in on the plan too and told to act as normal at all times and not to be laughin' and give the game away. So, durin' the course of the night they kept everything natural enough and when the night was wearin' on and Willie was startin' to drop hints about the tay, one a the boys stared over at Willie for a bit and then quickly looked away again, tryin' not to be too bare faced about it so that Willie wouldn't be suspicious. Then he would stare at Willie again, a bit longer this time, and then a while later the other boy would do the same and duntin' his mate with the elbow 'til Willie realised that something was wrong.'

'Boys, Sandy, I think that I would a burst out laughin'! How did everyone keep a straight face anyway?' asked Paddy.

'I don't know how they did it, Paddy, but they did, and managed to pull it off! Anyway Willie realised that somethin' was up and said, 'Are youse alright boys?'

'Oh aye, we're alright,' one of them said, 'just a bit worried that's all. It might be nothin' at all, Willie.'

'What might be nothin' at all?' asked Willie.

'We don't like the colour a ye, Willie, that's all,' said one boy.

'What's wrong with me colour anyway?'

'You're very jaundiced lookin', Willie,' said one a the boys 'If I was all jaundiced like that I would be all worried about it.'

'There's nothin' wrong with me colour at all,' said Willie, 'and I feel as fit as a fiddle.'

'Aye but that's the way it goes,' said the other boy, 'you don't notice it yourself at first til it gets a big grip on ye. It's only others that notice it. I knew a man that had the same thing and denied that he had it and now he's kickin' up the daisies.'

'For God's sake what are youse talkin' about?' said Willie, startin' to get a bit worried looking now. 'What are ye's sayin' is wrong with me anyway?'

'We're not sayin' you have anythin' bad at all, Willie, but it would be worth gettin' yourself looked at anyway, just in case, before it would be too late.'

'I've just remembered,' said the other boy, 'it was too much tannin that killed the man we were just tellin' you about…. over exposure to tannin.'

'What's tannin anyway?' asked Willie.

'It's the stuff that's in the tay Willie. Sure the tay leaves are loaded with it and too much of it is rale bad for ye…..a rale killer ye know…. get yourself looked at Willie, before it's too late. We wouldn't want to be sendin' for the minister now would we?'

'Oh now,' said the other boy, 'I hope it never comes to that. It would be an awful shame for that to happen.'

'Ah not at all … there's a lot a things they can do for the tannin poisonin' these days. There's things they can give ye to hold it back and give ye a lot more years de ye know….. as long as ye stay off the tay.'

'Boys Sandy' said Paddy, 'that must a put the wind up Willie!'

'Well he was startin' to fidget about at that stage and as far as I heard he seemed to have stopped the hintin' about the tay bein' made. Then he got up and started to look at himself in one a them big mirrors that was hangin' above the mantle piece.'

'A think it's only the way the light a the lamp's shinin' on me that's makin' me a bit out a colour,' said Willie, startin' to believe that there was somethin' wrong.

'It's nothin' to do with the light a the lamp,' said one of the boys, 'sure you're as yellow as a dockin root…. how much tay are ye drinkin' anyway?'

'Not that much,' said Willie, 'and sure I've been drinkin' tay all me life an' me father before me and it hasn't done us any harm before.'

'Aye but the tay leaves are comin' from a different part a the world nowadays, Willie,' said one of the boys, 'far stronger than what we used to get before… much more tannin in them. Sure they're that strong, if you've ever noticed, the tay spoon nearly stands up in the cup by itself. Cut it down Willie or maybe you would be better without the tay at all?'

'Maybe a should lave it for a while anyway,' said Willie, 'just in case.'

'You're a wise man, Willie …,' said the other boy, '…. a very wise man. We wouldn't want to lose you now would we?' and everyone in the house agreed.

'A sup a butter milk is rale good for the stomach,' somebody said, 'rale good…. and it helps to bring your colour back as well.'

'Have youse any in the house?' said Willie, 'I could do with a mug of it now. I'll take a sup now if youse have it' and someone brought Willie a porringer of buttermilk. 'Ah sure that bates the tay any day….buttermilk an' spuds, sure we were all reared on it anyway. There's none a that oul tannin youse are talkin' about in buttermilk' and then Willie got up to go home and there wasn't a word about tay bein' made after that.

'Boys Sandy!' said Paddy, 'did Willie ever go to the doctor about the tannin? The doctor would a took some look at him if he had heard a story like that.'

'I think, Paddy, that he talked about it to somebody else and they must a told him someone was havin' him on but it worked anyway for I heard he stayed away from that house and I suppose he would a been afraid to mention the tay anyway. He would a been too embarrassed and stayed away.'

> You'll take a sup a tay before lavin'
> Just a wee drop in your hand
> A piece a fadge bread an butter
> A scouder a made on the pan

Glossary:
Tay – tea
Scouder - flat white bread
Fadge - homemade soda bread
Porringer - tin mug

Fermanagh's Teenage Writing Sensation in 1927 – Myrtle Johnston
by John Cunningham

Magheramena Castle, about three miles from Belleek was the home of Myrtle Johnston, a teenage writing prodigy who became a bestselling author in the 1920s. One of her ancestors on her mother's side was the notable Irish author, Maria Edgeworth. Myrtle is one of the few Fermanagh authors to achieve this notable distinction. Her sister, Marjorie is much less well known but also remarkably, at the age of 18, published a biography of Napoleon. Myrtle's famous book was entitled "Hanging Johnny" and was first published in 1927.

Magheramena Castle

It was reviewed by the American magazine "Time" on Monday, April 30, 1928.

HANGING JOHNNY—Myrtle Johnston—Appleton ($2). For a handful of silver, Johnny the Hangman hangs his friend, knowing him innocent. The horror of it clings, though Johnny escapes the indignant mob to a distant Irish village. He foreswears his occupation, and, a lover of love and beauty falls in love with an affectionate but unimaginative woman. Practical, ambitious, Anna persuades her moonraking Johnny to earn occasional hangman's fees, and bring home the dead man's things, now a decent coat, now a stout pair of boots. Tortured by this necessity, Johnny broods over his ropes and ring, croons the ugly details to a fascinated small son, demonstrating with a grotesque rag doll on a miniature scaffold. In a drunken brawl at the inn Johnny champions a slattern, more unfortunate even than himself, befriends her, loves her, kills her jealous brute of a husband. She is convicted of the murder, and Johnny hangs her, dooming himself to tragedy. Author Johnston shows no trace of youthfulness in the grim story she tells with relentless force, compassion, and restraint. She is 18.

Back in Ireland the book also received a very enthusiastic review by J. S. Crone (*Irish Book Lover*, 1928): '*Hanging Johnny* (Murray) is one of the shortest and most original works of fiction I have ever read. There are practically only three characters: the hangman, his wife, and a half-mad priest, and the attention is gripped in the first paragraph, and held enthralled to the last. Yet I am told the author, Myrtle Johnson, is only eighteen years old. If this be so, she is a genius.'

The last of the Johnston succession of Magheramena Castle, Belleek, was James Cecil Johnston. He is described as of Magheramena Castle and Glencore House nearby. He was High Sheriff of Fermanagh in 1910 and served as Lieutenant, with the 14th Hussars in South Africa. He was Deputy Ranger of the Curragh of Kildare from 1910 and Master of the Horse to His Excellency the Lord Lieutenant of Ireland, Lord Aberdeen, from the same date. John Hamilton-Gordon, 1st Marquess of Aberdeen and Temair, (3 August 1847 – 7 March 1934) was known as The Earl of Aberdeen from 1870 to 1916. He was a Scottish politician, born in Edinburgh and held office in several countries, serving twice as Lord Lieutenant of Ireland (1886; 1905–1915) and from 1893 to 1898 as the seventh Governor General of Canada.

James Cecil Johnston was born in 1880 and married on the 28th of October 1903 Violet Myrtle Waters, daughter of S. A. Walker Waters, Assistant Inspector General of the Royal Irish Constabulary. There were three daughters: Myrtle, born 7th March 1909, Marjorie Helen, born January 18th 1911 and Mary who died at a young age. James Cecil Johnston was killed in the Dardanelles Campaign in 1916 at Suvla Bay when a Turkish shell exploded beside a group of three in conversation. Colonel F. A. Greer, C. O. lost an arm and R. S. Trimble of Enniskillen's Impartial Reporter was shell-shocked but both recovered.

The family fortunes had been in decline for some time particularly as a result of a prolonged legal dispute over land and after his death the Magheramena Estate had to be sold. The castle was briefly occupied by the IRA in 1922. The Roman Catholic Parish bought the Castle in a piece of clerical grandioseness as a residence for the Parish Priest and it's first occupant was Fr Lorcan O'Kieran, an ardent Republican and the man reputed to have coined the name Sinn Fein; an attribution also made to Cahir Healy, the Fermanagh politician and writer. He resided there until his death except for a brief period in 1922 when he was evicted by a force of A Specials just prior to the capture of Belleek in June of that year. Fr. O'Kieran had presided over Republican Courts in the Castle during this period. The castle was sadly unroofed by a clerical successor who according to local lore made a handsome financial present of it to Barney (Mr) Eastwood in just the lead of the roof alone.

The wife and children of James Cecil Johnston moved firstly to Blackrock near Dublin and after partition, which they had bitterly opposed, they moved to Bournemouth in England. There Myrtle Johnston achieved fame as an author but although she continued to write she never achieved the fame and acclaim of her first book.

In Stanley Kunitz, 20th Century Authors, 1942, and Report of 1956 we get Myrtle Johnston's life to date as recorded by her. "I was born, the eldest of three sisters, in Dublin. Our branch of the Johnston family had come from Annandale, Scotland, to Ireland during the persecution of the Covenanters in the seventeenth century, one of them building Magheramena Castle on the shores of Lough Erne in the beautiful, but wild and desolate, County Fermanagh. We were the last of his descendants to inhabit the Castle. My father, Captain James Johnston, was Master of the Horse, and later private secretary to Lord Aberdeen during his second term as Lord Lieutenant of Ireland. My mother, the daughter of an Irish District Inspector of Police, and one of ten sisters celebrated in Irish society as 'the ten lovely Miss Waterses,' was, like my father, an ardent Nationalist. 'Ireland' and 'Home Rule' are words I remember early attending to in grown-up conversation at the Private Secretary's Lodge.

Maria Edgeworth

"I was six when my father was killed at the Dardanelles in 1915. Left without the means to keep on Magheramena, my mother sold it and for the next five years, the most formative for me as an author, we lived in Dublin. Before I could read I had determined that I would write stories. It became my abiding purpose. At ten, I received my first rejection from a magazine, the London Windsor. I continued writing stories, poems, and plays— most historical or fantastic—often submitting my work to magazines, but never being in the least cast down by rejection, which I almost welcomed as an inevitable part of the business of becoming an author. My family was in no sense literary—although an ancestor was Maria Edgeworth, so celebrated in her day and so forgotten in ours—and we knew no writers, so that I pursued my ambition happily, without criticism, influence, or advice.

"Not long before my twelfth birthday, the Irish Troubles of 1920-21—that betrayal of Nationalist dreams—decided my mother to follow the example of nearly all our friends and leave Ireland for England, where we have since lived quietly in Bournemouth, Dorset. I did not go to boarding school or university. In Ireland we had had governesses, and in Bournemouth we attended a small P.N.E.U. day school which I left at seventeen.

"At fifteen, I sent my first full-length novel to a publisher. It was turned down, and so was my second, although with very kindly encouragement from the London firm which accepted my third novel, Hanging Johnny—my first published work—when I was eighteen. Three other novels and a volume of short stories followed. I was deflected, in those years, from the straight path to a measure of financial and literary success, which my first book had seemed to indicate, by a desire to experiment with form and subject which I fear has not left me yet. Having begun early to publish,

I regard much of my work as the cast-off clothes of a growing child, bearing little relation, perhaps, to any ultimate achievement of mine.

"My second sister Marjorie was, also at eighteen, the author of a commentary on certain episodes of Napoleonic history entitled Domination.

Principal Works : Hanging Johnny, 1927; Relentless, 1930; The Maiden, 1935; Laleen and Other Stories, 1938; The Rising, 1939; Amiel, 1941.

In the follow up report of 1956 she tells of her current life.
"Myrtle Johnston writes from Canford Cliffs, Dorset: "My eyesight is bad and prevented my enlisting in the Auxiliary Territorial Service in 1942. I therefore spent the War years working in a branch of the Home Office which had a responsibility for organizing the civil side of the military preparations for the invasion of Normandy. During this period I deliberately ceased to be a creative writer. My first post-war novel, A Robin Redbreast in a Cage, a dramatic inquiry into the nature of guilt and crime, won a recommendation from the British Book Society and was published in 1951 in the United States. I have just finished writing 'Lorelle,' a modern love story with a poetic theme, which I hope soon to publish [1952]."
Additional Work : A Robin Redbreast in a Cage, 1950.

This, Myrtle Johnston's second last novel, received a fairly critical slating as in this Sunday Times review of 4th June, 1950.
"Some years before the last war 18-year-old Myrtle Johnston, whose home is at Bournemouth, wrote a book, a dramatic story called "Hanging Johnny", which became a best seller. It was a good book. She followed with other novels, then decided she was not writing up to her own critical standards. For about 10 years she wrote nothing. Now she has returned to the literary scene with "A Robin Redbreast in a Cage" (Heinemann. 9s. 6d.), which, if it does nothing else, shows its author is still searching for something, but for what is not clear.

It is a queer story. It cannot be classified as a thriller, nor is it purely a dramatic romance. It is a restless, uneasy excursion into the minds of two people. A young man is acquitted of murdering a tramp, because the tramp, injured by society, seems to him the symbol of an even greater menace to it. He is cleared on false evidence given by a forgotten schoolmate who has always idolised him. The scene moves to a squalid setting where the young man becomes acquainted with, and,, in his strange way, enamoured of, a girl, who, because of a vicious sin committed against her, becomes a prison officer so that she can make and watch others suffer.

I read on in the hope of discovering what the author was trying to prove. She proves nothing, and her story gets nowhere. This time I fear that all that can be said is that Miss Johnston has written an aimless, certainly a depressing, and undoubtedly a pointless, story, saved, perhaps by its distinctive writing. G.Y.

In 1986 I wrote a letter to the Bournemouth "Evening Echo" seeking information about Myrtle Johnston and the rest of the family. I received the following reply from a lady who knew the family well. Hers is the only known personal record of the Johnston family in self-imposed "exile."

Sarum,
11, Rowland's Hill,
Wimborne,
Dorset BH 21 1ALI
27 October 1986.

Dear Mr. Cunningham,
I am writing in answer to your letter printed in the Bournemouth 'Evening Echo' on Saturday, 18 October. Just over a year ago I answered a similar letter from a Dr. Gridgeman of British Columbia who was interested in Myrtle Johnston's younger sister Marjorie. He is a collector of books on Napoleon and apparently Marjorie wrote his biography in 1930 when she also was only about 18.

I knew the Johnston family who, according to Kelly's Directory lived in Ravine Road, Canford Cliffs, Dorset from at least 1923 to 1930. In 1932 they moved to Maxwell Road close by and are still listed at that address until 1950. Both houses were called 'The Myrtles'.

I was born in Canford Cliffs, which is now in Poole but was then considered to be part of West Bournemouth, but we moved in about 1923 so I don't know when our acquaintance with the family began. I don't think my father was their doctor but I believe the youngest of the three girls Mary, went to the P.N.E.U. School in Westbourne, Bournemouth where I also went.

There were three girls and a mother and they were a charming family. I don't remember Mrs. Johnston, but I fancy she was slim and very feminine whereas Myrtle and Marjorie were distinctly on the plump side, Myrtle having also a rather 'plummy' voice. She was rather aloof, but this was probably because she was about 10 years older than me. Marjorie was cheerful and friendly and very good with children. Mary was tall and quiet. I believe she died young.

We used to meet on the beach at about the time that Myrtle came to fame with her book 'Hanging Johnny' which was considered very astonishing for a girl of her age. I never read it of course. I had no idea that Marjorie wrote. I did not know that they came from Ireland and I don't recall that they had anything but an upper class English accent.

I have a post card somewhere of the Ravine Road house which I was given as second prize in a sandcastle competition (if I remember rightly). I can send you this if I can find it and will also send a xerox copy of a newspaper cutting of 1950 with a picture of Myrtle and a rather lukewarm review of her book 'A Robin Redbreast' published by Heinemann. I only remember going to the Maxwell Road house once, which must have been after 1932, and this is odd as I was at a boarding school in the next road. Mrs. Johnston's initials are given as V. M. I don't know if she was a widow, but I never saw her husband or heard of him.

From 1942-47 their name is missing from the Directory and possibly they left for a while as Canford Cliffs was practically on the cliff top. This residential area might well have been cleared, or the houses requisitioned during this period. By 1947 they were back again. It is interesting that a Mr. William Allen Johnson (sic) is listed in the directory of 1922-1933 at 'The Myrtles", 56 Richmond Wood Road. This is in north central Bournemouth. He is not there in 1942.

I wonder why the family was so obsessed with the letter 'M' and in particular with Myrtles? Is there something Irish about this? I believe Belleek is where that very pretty porcelain is made. I do hope the enclosed will be of interest to you. I would like to know of your final discoveries and what is the family's connection with Magheramena Castle as I cannot find their name in the Landed Gentry of Ireland. Perhaps Mrs. V. M. Johnston came from there.

Best wishes in your work
Yours sincerely

(Miss) Betty Matthews.

NOTE. - A PNEU School means that it is affiliated to the Parents' National Education Union (PNEU). There are PNEU Schools throughout the British Isles and the world. PNEU Schools have always been known to have a well structured and wide curriculum. The movement started towards the end of the 19th century, influenced by the principles and ideas of a renowned Victorian educationalist, Charlotte Mason, who died in 1923. She founded the Charlotte Mason Teacher Training College in the Lake District, to train students in her philosophy and methods, as well as all other aspects of education. Her ideas challenged the generally accepted views of how to educate children. She believed that "children are persons", and that teachers and parents should treat them as individuals who need to be stimulated from an early age by a broad curriculum, not simply to be trained to read, write and count. That curriculum should contain the best literature, the best art, the best contemporary science etc. At the end of the 20th century these ideas may seem self-evident; they were not self-evident at the end of the 19th century and it could be argued that it is only because of Charlotte Mason and others like her that they are regarded as self-evident now.

None of the Johnston girls married as far as is known nor do family records seem to have survived. Myrtle's death is recorded at Poole, Dorset in 1955 aged 46 years. The fact that they left Ireland seems to have had the effect of obliterating the memory of this talented literary family. It is hoped that this article may restore them to the collective memory of Fermanagh.

It is hard to imagine where Myrtle Johnston sourced her knowledge of hanging but perhaps from another Fermanagh author, Charles Duff of Enniskillen, who produced a best seller in 1923; four years before Myrtle's book. This was "*A handbook on hanging*". In the New York Review of Books, 1961 the 196 page book is described as "*a Swiftian tribute to that unappreciated mainstay of civilization: the hangman. With barbed insouciance, Charles Duff writes not only of hanging but of electrocution, decapitations, and gassings; of innocent men executed and of executions botched; of the bloodlust of mobs and the shabby excuses of the great. This coruscating and, in contemporary America, very relevant polemic makes clear that whatever else capital punishment may be said to be – justice, vengeance a deterrent – it is certainly killing*"

Myrtle Johnston in later life

The following is the first chapter of Hanging Johnny; the 1920s best seller, to give a flavour of the writing of a talented Fermanagh teenager:

The interior of the scaffold house grew suddenly brighter, as the sun broke through a bank of clouds, sending a triumphant shaft of light through a chink in the wall.

As if he sensed the sudden brightness, the condemned man lifted his head and a suggestion of hope came over his haggard figure.

"Will you take this white bag off of my eyes?" he said hoarsely.

For a moment no one answered.

The sheriff, the Governor and the others who were there to watch him die were looking towards the tiny spear of light, in a sudden silence. Only the executioner held his head down and fidgeted with the pinioning straps round the man's legs.

Then the surgeon said gently: "It is better not."

"You brutes!" the man shouted. "Will you be denying me a last sight of the day?"

There was a desperate sob in his voice.

The chaplain stepped forward.

"No one denies you that, Tim Derrybawn," he said, and plucked off the white cap so that the man's face was exposed, brave, pale, excited, lifted eagerly to the sun. The executioner came forward very slowly and began to adjust the rope. His hand faltered a little as he slipped the ring behind the left ear. Then he put his hand on the bolt and the chaplain's voice rose thrillingly clear and impassioned in the last prayers for the dead.

"Wait!" cried the condemned man, "wait!"

The chaplain paused—he was saying the prayers, not reading them—and the executioner, with a look of something like hope, took his hand from the lever.

"What is the meaning of this?" said the sheriff.

"The reprieve! They'll be sending the reprieve, and God help us all if it comes too late." The prisoner's eyes were alight and he strained forward in the leather straps.

"This is the way he does be talking all the day," one of the warders whispered to the chaplain. "Always thinking of that reprieve he is. On the way from the cell he says to me: 'They can't delay with it any longer,' he says. But sure your reverence knows the way he does be talking. If it wasn't that I was in court, and heard the evidence with my two ears, I'd be thinking myself it was not Tim Derrybawn who knifed Peter Connor in the club at Daly's."

A look of profound pity came into the chaplain's eyes. He bent towards the sheriff.

"We might wait," he said in a low voice.

"Not a scrap of use. The Home Office wouldn't consider his appeal for a moment. At his trial, his guilt was established beyond any doubt. The man Job Moran, especially, gave damning evidence. Poor devil, he's probably trying to gain time."

"Is it letting an innocent man die they are?" said the condemned man, and a slight fear showed in his voice.

Someone, one of the warders perhaps, gave a short laugh and the man's face blazed red.

"Found guilty, I was, in the court, and me as innocent as yourself, your honour. I swore in court, and I swear now, that I didn't kill Peter Connor. But sure, I couldn't say the things I wanted the way they did be asking me questions and argueing with each other. If they'd made me think I was guilty at the end of it all, there'd be no wonder in it at all."

"The hypnotism of a cross-examination" murmured the chaplain under his breath. The sheriff opened his lips, but the man with the rope round his neck broke in again fiercely, vehemently.

"Peter Connor was a dirty dog of an informer, so he was, and I'd have liked mighty well to wring the lying throat of him. But I kept my hands off him, and it's the truth, as God sees me, that I don't know who it was knifed him that night over Daly's pub. I had the drink taken, God help me."

The sheriff stepped up to the executioner, who stood fingering an old, charred piece of rope he had taken from his pocket, his eyes still sullen and downcast.

"Better get it over quickly," said the sheriff in a whisper. "The man's raving. He's only trying to gain time."

The hangman moved slowly across to the lever again putting back the old piece of rope. His head was still bent, and he walked in a curious shambling way. The prisoner turned to him, straining forward in his leather bonds. The colour had died off his face, leaving it white and panic stricken.

"Johnny, you hypocrite!" he said huskily. "Begging me to confess in the cell, you were, the way you'd be sure you wouldn't be hanging an innocent man, and knowing all the while I was as innocent as my own child."

The hangman lifted his head as if he were going to speak. Then he looked away from the desperate eyes of the other man and said nothing.

"Me that was your friend," said Tim Derrybawn, "the only friend you had in the whole of this town. I wish I'd never taken up with you at all, so I do. Sure, didn't everyone in this town but myself know that there's no good in a man who does work the like of yours."

The warders and the surgeon's assistants were gaping at the singularity of the scene. It was like no other they had ever witnessed. The chaplain took a step forward and stretched out his arm to the prisoner, pointing his emaciated forefinger. It was a curious attitude, almost one of power and prophecy. "Surrender yourself, Tim Derrybawn," he said. "Even now the Powers are preparing to avenge you and those who have suffered like you. And you perhaps are already the last in the world to die by the will of mankind."

There was a silence of amazement and bewilderment as the chaplain stepped back to his place. Even as they stared at him, wondering if they had really heard him speak, the light died out of his eyes, and his tall, gaunt figure seemed to shrink into itself again.

But, as the condemned man listened, a sort of fierce resignation came over his face.

"You're killing an innocent man," he said slowly, " and may God forgive you for it. Things the like of this shouldn't be let happen."

He turned his haggard eyes to the executioner.

"The curse of Heaven fail on you, Hanging Johnny, for the murder that's on your soul. For it's murder you're doing before God and the Saints. There's them outside will have your blood for this."

The hangman's hand faltered on the lever, and he let go his grasp on it.
"Slide that bolt and be damned to you," cried Tim Derrybawn. "I'm not afraid to die. There's no sin on my soul, and my God knows I am innocent."

The chaplain stepped forward, as if he were going to protest. Then he restrained himself and recited the last words of the prayer for the dead.

The hangman seized the bolt and it swung backwards with a heavy crash. The trap-doors under Tim Derrybawn's feet fell open.

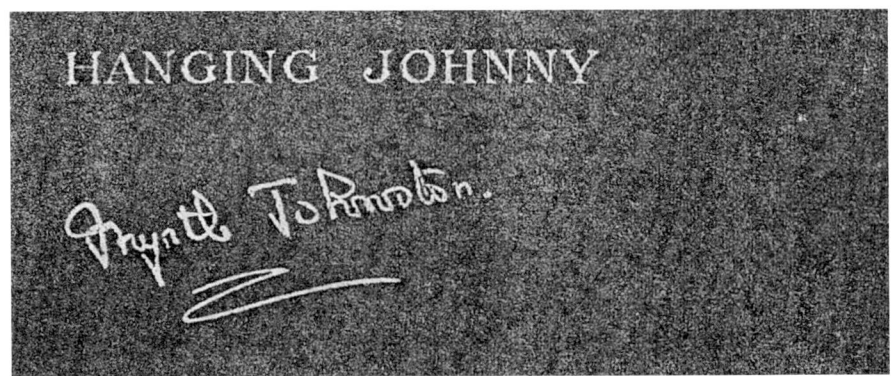

Myrtle Johnston's signature

Unbound
by Mary Montague

I have unbuckled my ornate
scold's bridle. My tongue
is sore from the bit. It roams
my mouth's hollow, soft muscle
to test the edge of a bite. While
my mind turns on my mother's
last words, my tongue holds
back. The time for speech is past.
I have to act. And every move
is checkmate as my fingers unpick
the knots, my teeth gnaw
through tangles. My back straightens.
My eyes are level with yours. Watch
now for the wink of my heels as I walk away.

Repair
by Mary Montague

Petals have dropped pink and white,
a crinkled brown-edged confetti,
from fading blooms onto the worn
kitchen table. My mother
hesitates; reaches her aged
hand, the skin a loose garment
on the frame of bones; gathers
the petals; dabs them gently,
carefully, back onto dying
blossoms. How conscientiously,
correctly, she matches colour
for colour, my mother,
reaching back, mending
her flowers, *too late, too late.*

3 Letterboy Road
by Mary Montague

Now the house is bone-beautiful, laved, balmed.
The smoothness of the blank and tranquil walls
soothes my hand. Surfaces are scoured; carpets
steamed; the curtains dry-cleaned; nets and linings
washed; everything re-hung. Nicotine
no longer haunts the air. The kitchen's space
is blanched with sunshine. The burner hums
(I have learned, at last, how to set
the timer). To visit now is near-
relief: all smells warm, fresh, cared-for.
I could not wash your body; I could not
lay you out; but I have done this:
I have left these rooms rinsed, empty
and at rest; their bare grace full of light.

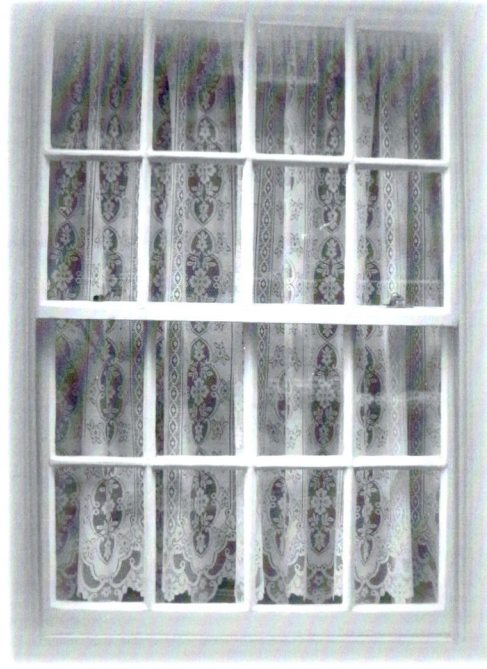

The Dinner Girl
by John Reihill

It was a very humid evening in late July, when Mrs McBurny asked her teenage daughter Susan who was home on holiday from college, if she would take the dinner over to Pat Muldoon, who lived a few hundred meters across the fields from their house.

Mrs. McBurny had been bringing dinner to Pat for over two years now. It started when Pat's wife died suddenly of a heart attack at the age of 68, leaving Pat on his own.

They had two married daughters living about 10 miles distant in different directions. They also had a son who went off to Australia in a huff after having a row with his Father over some task on the farm.

The daughters and their families visited him quite often, but couldn't be there every day. The son had not been heard of since he left home many years ago. Although they knew where he went they had no address for him.

On reaching 70 years old, a few years before his wife's death Pat had decided to quit farming, and had leased the farm to his neighbour James McBurny. Although they mearned each other they were in different townlands, and a wide drain separated them.

For the McBurnys to get to Muldoon's house they had to go down their own lane to the road, turn right and go down the road for about a quarter of a mile, turn right again into a winding lane that led to Muldoon's house and farmyard.

After James McBurny leased Muldoon's farm he put a strong plank across the mearn drain, so that he could get to the farmyard more easily. This was the route Mrs. McBurny took when bringing the dinner over to Pat. Susan would take the same route now.

Pat was an affable old man, and invited Susan to come in and sit down for a while. He hadn't seen her since she was home last Easter.

As the two of them sat chatting the sky darkened. Soon a wicked flash of lightening lit up the kitchen, and was immediately followed by a tremendous brattle of thunder that shook the house. By God that was a close one, said Pat, looking towards Susan who had went deathly pale. No sooner had he spoken, than a torrent of rain came lashing down. The guttering was unable to take the water as it rushed from the slated roof of the house to cascade to the ground like a waterfall.

The rain and thunder continued, and Susan phoned her Mother to say that she wouldn't go home until the storm cleared; she would be safe with Pat.

As she was about to hang up the phone she realised that it had went dead. The line must have got struck by the lightening.

Meantime Pat's daughter Margaret Brown was worried about her Father in the storm, and decided to phone him to find out if he was safe, or if the storm was as bad with him as it was where she lived. The line was dead and she couldn't get through to him; this added to her worries.

Her husband had gone to a farmers' meeting in the parochial hall or he might have driven over to Pat's place to see if he was safe.

Just then she heard the Landrover pull up in the yard, and a few seconds later her youngest son John dashed into the house, making a comment about the terrible evening it was. "Indeed it is," said his mother. "I was trying to get through to Daddy on the phone, but the line is down, I'm very worried about him".

"I'll go over to him in the Landrover," said John, "although the roads are flooded in many places the rover will make it. I think the worst of the storm is over".

John had just arrived home from his work with the Forestry Commission. After a hurried dinner, which his Mother had ready for him, he set out for his Grandfather's house. It took him longer than he had thought it would, as there was a lot of flooding on the road, and there were still some heavy showers falling. Although the thunder had moved away, he could still see an odd flash of lightening against the sky.

When he finally arrived at his Grandfather's house and went in he found him safe and well in the company of a very attractive young girl.

His Grandfather introduced him to the girl saying this is James McBurny's daughter Susan; she had just arrived with the dinner to me when the storm broke and decided to remain here until it settled.

After the introduction Susan asked the young man if he would like a cup of tea. John replied that he would as he had a hurried dinner before leaving home.

All the while Susan was preparing the tea John could not keep his eyes off her. Surely this very attractive young girl could not be the long legged, skinny girl he chased out of his Grandfather's orchard a few years ago when he found her stealing apples, if so he hoped that she hadn't remembered it. At the time when he told his Grandfather about it, he replied, oh that would be James McBurny's daughter Susan, she won't do any harm, she only takes an odd apple or pear that she eats, and usually tells me about it.

By this time the storm had passed over so Susan said she would head for home. "I don't think I will cross the fields," she said. "There may be a flood in the drain." "Indeed there is," said Pat. "I was looking out a while ago and the fields are flooded, and I expect the foot stick may be swept away."

At this point John spoke up. 'I will be going home immediately. My Mother will be worried about Granda, and as he is safe and well looked after there is no need for me to stay any longer. I can give you a lift in the rover. I will be passing your lane anyhow.' Susan accepted the offer and John dropped her at the end of her lane.

As Susan entered the house, her Mother spoke and said she was glad to see her home safely. "Did you come round by the road?" she asked, "I expect the fields are flooded!" They are indeed, replied Susan; Pat was looking out and said they were flooded, and that the foot stick is probably swept away. One of his grandsons had come up to see if he was safe from the storm. He brought me to the end of the lane in his Landrover. Her Father spoke up and said that would be John Brown, he works for the forestry commission. He's a nice lad I have met him a few times when he was visiting Pat.

Next day the flood had subsided and when James McBurny went out to inspect the foot stick he found that it had indeed been swept away. He found it on higher ground in the next field and with the help of his two boys they dragged it back and got it repositioned across the drain.

Susan volunteered to bring the dinner to James every evening during the holiday period, and even told her Mother one day that she was going over to iron James's shirts. He had spoken to her about ironing his shirts and remarked that he didn't make a great job of it. "Kate, happy rest to her, always did those jobs, and could do it well. You know I miss her a lot," he said.

Towards the end of the holiday season Susan announced that she wouldn't go back to College. "I didn't get a great pass and it's probably a waste of time and money if I went back," she said. Her parents encouraged her to continue for another year and that maybe she would do better this time, but it was her decision. She said she would take a year out anyhow and take it from there. She would look for a job in Dunne's stores in the local town.

She did get a job in Dunne's stores and cycled in to work every day. If she was on the early shift and had evenings off she would volunteer to bring the dinner over to Pat. Her young brothers would sometimes be over with their Father on Pat's place helping him to move cattle or some light chore. It was obvious that they had seen Susan and John Brown together on a few occasions. Sometimes if they wanted to tease her they would start singing John Brown's Body.

One evening after James had been over at Pat's place he remarked to his wife. "John Brown seems to be paying a lot of attention to his Grandfather lately; I suppose he will inherit the place".

"I think it is our daughter that he is paying attention to," replied his wife. James just gave a tut tut and changed the subject.

A short time after that Susan became rather morose and then one evening she said to her Mother "I wont be bringing the dinner to Pat this evening, maybe you or some of the boys could bring it over." Her Mother looked at her and asked, "Are you not feeling well or is there something wrong?" "I'm alright, Mum" she replied. When her Mother questioned her farther as to what might be wrong, she snapped back "leave me alone, Mum, I'm all right." The Mother seemed to sense what was wrong and dropped the subject.

It was a week or more later when Susan was on the early shift and home early that she announced that she would bring the dinner over to Pat, saying that he might want some ironing done, it is a couple of weeks since I last ironed shirts for him.

Her mother had Pat's dinner ready and Susan set off in high spirits to deliver it. Truth was John Brown had called into the supermarket to see her that day, and whatever difference there had been between them it was ironed out, and they were now going to meet at Pat's place.

Later that evening John Brown left Susan home in the Landrover, and soon he was a regular caller at the house.

One evening when he left Susan home he loitered outside the door for a while. When Susan's Mother asked, "Are you not coming in"? He replied "No, I'm in a hurry home this evening. Mammy's Cousins from America are visiting us in a couple of week's time and she is doing up the house in preparation for them. She has some heavy furniture to move and asked me to help her this evening. We will be having a party some night for them. Would it be alright for Susan to come to the party? I can pick her up and leave her home again. Granda will be coming also."

"If Susan wants to go we have no objection, Pat will keep an eye on her for us," the Mother replied.

One evening the following week Susan and John arrived at the house together. As soon as they entered the kitchen Susan bolted to the bedroom. John stood inside the door looking very uncomfortable. Mrs McBurny asked him to come in and have a seat. John declined saying that he would not be stopping long, and it would not be worth while sitting down. After edging about inside the doorway and looking more uncomfortable he finally blurted out, "I want to marry Susan, with your consent of course." James looked him up and down for quite a while and then said with a grin on his face, "I thought you were supposed to bring a bottle of whiskey on an occasion like this."

"Sorry sir," replied John, "I'm not much of a drinker myself and I never thought of it." James and his wife stared at each other for a while, and then nodded in unison to each other. "Have you spoken to Susan yet?" asked Mrs McBurny. John said that he had, "but she wouldn't give me an answer until I got your consent".

Mrs Mc Burny called her daughter from the room. "This young man says he wants to marry you, but do you want to marry him?" "Yes I do," replied a red faced Susan. "In that case," said her mother, "we have no objection. He is a decent young man, and we know his family well, but we think you are a bit young yet."

John now spoke up with more confidence. First he thanked the McBurnys for their consent and kind words. "We don't intend to marry for a couple of years yet. I am in line for promotion at work next year and Granddad is leaving me the farm. We will be living in with him, so Susan won't be moving far from home".

"The party for Mammy's cousins will be next Friday week. You are all welcome to come to it."

"I thought you were never going to ask us," said James. "I haven't seen your Mother or her sister since your Granny's death. Roll on Friday week."

The Lammasman, born August First 1930
by Sean McElgunn

Back down the Finn and up the Erne
The moon had slid by Ramper brae
They stole among the coot and tern
Their pirate hoard white bread and tay - 1940

Again last night that curlew-call
Once more he asked - why did you die?
The red-haired duke best-loved of all
It's lonesome here in Athenry - 1950

A paradise this tropic isle
What better life - the Lord's commando
Among his own this little while
He sometimes dreams he's back on Ando - 1960

A glorious place was Antrim's coast
No mindless strife in calm Glenarm
The dream was shattered by the ghost
He fled once more in wild alarm - 1970

Still searching for he knew not what
Was this what life was meant to be?
Alike unsure to go or not
Alone or in good company? - 1980

Year upon year he waited on fate
No lodestar yet that he could see
By purist chance he met his mate
A kindred soul as lone as he - 1990

Man's full of smarts and full of folly
Come rain, come shine they've stuck together
Why should life be melancholy?
Soul-mates survive in any weather - 2000

The mute swans speak of living peace
The lough flings back the moon-drenched sky
Great God, will wonders never cease?
You are the star for steering by – 2010

Heritage On The High Street
by Dianne Trimble

Three rail companies served County Fermanagh until the middle of the twentieth century: the Clogher Valley Railway, the Great Northern Railway (Ireland) and the Sligo Leitrim & Northern Counties Railway. The last two of these services ceased on 30th September, 1957 leaving the areas between Clones, Omagh, Sligo and Bundoran without rail service. More than just a means of transport was lost when this happened.

"[The railway] was sort of a glue that glued the various towns together and [railway] people were very much respected. The railway was a way of life, something quite solid in the community," railway enthusiast, Selwyn Johnston said.

Although the railway was gone from the county, it was not forgotten. Railway enthusiasts collected and preserved memorabilia and former employees reminisced about their past.

Selwyn Johnston shares his passion for railways with his brothers, Gordon and Nigel. Since childhood they have collected memorabilia and almost a decade ago they turned their hobby into Headhunters Railway Museum.

The museum defies the institution's stereotypical image as a staid, airless building filled with musty relics. Headhunters combines a museum with a thriving barbershop. Located on Enniskillen's high street and celebrating its thirtieth anniversary this year, the business is run by Gordon and Nigel; Selwyn curates the museum.

In 1997 Enniskillen Library hosted a small exhibition of railway artefacts to commemorate the 40th anniversary of the closure of rail services in Fermanagh. Its success spurred the Johnstons and other rail enthusiasts to search for suitable and affordable premises to house a permanent display. When the search proved unsuccessful the Johnstons offered a small section of their barbershop to house a railway collection.

So, on the 45th anniversary of the closure of Fermanagh rail services, the museum opened. It has been growing ever since, moving into the room next door and then the next room until it has taken over most of the building's first floor.

"When it first started in 2002 we never envisaged that it would go to this stage. So it has expanded which is great to see," Selwyn said. "We're not a museum, per se, like Fermanagh County Museum or Ulster Museum. But, I think, increasingly people are realising there is a place for this - where people who are like minded, who have an interest and a passion for a particular thing, want to create

The Railway Clock

a repository of items and [provide] that experience and that education."

Visitors climbing the stairs to the first floor museum find an authentic Railway Booking Office on the landing. I resisted the urge to ask the ticket collector mannequin, sitting at the counter, what the fare was. Museum admission is free and, although they are a registered charity, the enterprise is wholly funded by the barbershop and donations, without grant aid.

The museum houses a diverse collection from the railways and their associated hotels. Glass cabinets display tickets and nippers, train timetables, stationmasters' watches and tableware. Larger items such as uniforms, posters, photographs, monogrammed chairs and rugs, and railway equipment, including weighing scales, telegraph equipment, a porter's bicycle, a complete signal box and a pedal cycle inspection trolley for checking the tracks, cover walls and fill floor space. Engine nameplates, sporting local place names such as Lough Erne, Lough Melvin and Hazelwood, mingle with old station signs admonishing: "Please don't spit in the carriages. It is offensive to other passengers" and "Please adjust your dress before leaving", reminding male passengers to do up their buttons before leaving the toilet.

A station manager's office, complete with bespoke office furniture, telegraph equipment and a cat by the fire, nestles beside the barbers' chairs. A painted station platform scene provides a realistic view out of its office window.

The Stationmaster's Office

The brothers like to keep their displays fresh and interesting. "We're always adding in new exhibits and linking up with our colleagues in other museums and looking out for things with a local connection," Selwyn explained.

The museum's purpose is to collect, preserve and interpret local railway heritage. Besides their own artefacts, they also have items on loan from various individuals and museums. They eagerly co-operate with other institutions to exchange materials and information.

"We're members of various bodies such as the Museums Council, the Association of Independent Museums and the Heritage Railway Association," Selwyn said. "We get calls from other museums to help with exhibitions…it's actually a two way thing and we work closely with a lot of museums. Fermanagh County Museum is a great advocate and a great supporter."

The Johnstons appreciate the help and advice, especially regarding artefact conservation, they receive from the larger museum and feel that the County Museum treats them as a partner rather than a rival.

In turn they support and promote the work of other institutions. For example,

The photo shows the Changing Rooms presenter, Lawrence Llewellyn-Bowen and his wife, Jackie with the three Johnston brothers (on right side of photo). The Johnston brothers are (left to right from beside Jackie) - Selwyn, Gordon and Nigel.

they encourage schools to experience the Railway Preservation Society's steam train rides from Belfast Central Station to the Ulster Transport Museum, Cultra.

Their mission includes entertaining and educating the community, hosting school and group visits, lending artefacts for class lessons and answering genealogical and other rail heritage enquiries.

And they are an attraction that entices visitors to Fermanagh. "We think we're contributing in a small way to tourism potential and growth," Selwyn said. The railways always promoted tourism, producing stunning posters painted by renowned artists such as Paul Henry. "People tend to think tourism only started with Northern Ireland Tourist Board, Fermanagh Council and Lakeland Visitors' Centre. Railways were promoting attractions for years. We have adverts going back to 1938 and 1910 where they were promoting Marble Arch Caves and Bundoran."

Increasingly the economic climate and budget cutbacks are forcing institutions to seek new ways to remain viable. It may seem strange to find a museum in a barbershop but Selwyn counters any reservations that are voiced, "It is actually quite an innovative way to bring heritage onto the high street…It's open five days a week, from 9am to 5.30pm. People come in when they want, there's no admission. If they wish to make a donation to the museum they can. It's not closed over the winter…You get 30-40 people coming in every day to get their hair cut, have a chat, recall memories. I suppose some museums would be delighted to have 30 or 40 people coming in every day".

The Johnstons joke that their idea may catch on and one day there will be a franchise of barbershops linked to museums. Hell's Kitchen Museum in Castlereagh, Co Roscommon combines a bar with a railway museum and many museums earn revenue from cafes. So, in future, affiliating with other businesses to fund museum activities may not be unusual.

Headhunters welcomes a wide range of visitors. Its unique setting is a novelty for some. Rail enthusiasts and Irish daytrippers stop in during visits to Enniskillen. And some visitors, who first came as children to get their hair cut, return as adults bringing their own children with them. "We've visitors come from all over the world. Railways is a subject matter which crosses all nationalities," Selwyn said.

As well as collecting artefacts, they also gather and preserve social history. "Over the years we've recorded the former railway employees' memories…We produced a CD – all the different things that they remember like the closure, what a [working] day was like. We've encouraged former rail employees to put pen to paper. Many have written books on their experiences. It's keeping it alive in many different ways. We're sentimental and people say it's sad it was closed. And we say yes, but we can't change time. But I suppose we can keep the memory alive and we can keep it in people's minds that this once operated. It was a way of life," Selwyn said.

Although it was an integral part of life until 1957, today's generation will never experience rail travel in Fermanagh. Trains in Fermanagh carried workers to their jobs; wartime evacuees from Belfast to the safety of the countryside; daytrippers to the city for shopping and sports matches; holidaymakers to Bundoran; pilgrims to Lough Derg; children, including Portora Royal School boarders from across Ireland, to school and on Sunday School excursions, and Belleek Pottery's products to shops.

Ticket Collector in his booth

It's fortunate that this heritage can still be experienced at Headhunters. Selwyn said, "We're expanding upstairs with Erne Model Railway Club. We've linked with them and we're creating an O gauge model railway layout using these fantastically hand built locomotives and carriages that actually run on the line. So it brings it to a whole new area now. It's all about increasing the interest in railways and keeping it alive."

Headhunters Museum and Barbershop is located at 5 Darling Street, Enniskillen, Co Fermanagh. Telephone: 028 6632 7488. Website: http://headhuntersmuseum.com.

Headhunters barbershop with railway displays

34

Roslea Wedding 1819
(recorded by Dermot Maguire)

In the year 1819
In sweet July
When leaves were green
There was a wedding held one day
Near to the town of Roslea

Of mountaineers I do protest,
There did assemble many a guest
And I was one among the rest.
Such a rabble came from Carnmore,
Above eleven and twenty score,
Of rich and poor, of old and young,
Of lame and blind, of deaf and dumb,
Collected there upon that day,
All dressed up, gaudy, fine and gay.

There was tinkers, barbers, brewers, bakers,
Cobblers, carpenters and brogue makers.
Gunners, hatters, wheelwrights and tailors,
Whitesmiths, gunsmiths, blacksmiths and nailors.
Bobbintossers, millers, doctors,
Gay old whistlers and tidy poeters,
Mudlarkers, noddinweavers and bogtrotters.
Slaters and pavers,
Fifty sets of sparrableweavers,
Bisom makers, cleavers,
Painters, hacklers, cutlers,
Coachmen, footmen, cooks and butchers.
Besides, to this assembly came,
A multitude I cannot name.
With harps and pipes and fiddles too,
They made a merry jovial crew.

They all got seated round about,
Ten dishes of colcannon and eight barrels of stout,
And at intervals they had at will,

Sour buttermilk to drink their fill,
That would take off (without a lie)
The pearl of a piper's eye.

Delicious food was next brought in,
Upon large vessels made of tin.
Lobsters, oysters and cow-heels,
Mussels, cockles, and fresh eels.
Trotters of sheep and half-boiled tripes,
Cranes and plovers, larks and snipes.

They then fell to it every man,
There was bloody work when they began,
Tripes and cow-heels to devour,
The like I never saw before
Or being demolished.
They now began to clear the tables everywhere.

The broken fragments they threw down,
Fin bones and shells upon the ground,
Whilst dogs and cats stood gaping all,
Waiting and ready for their fall,
And could devour them great and small.

While Pat stepped in with mystic pride,
His bonny blossom by his side.
He was dressed up both neat and trig,
He wore a double-breasted wig.
Beneath this wig a cape,
With a sooty fringe and cap.
A grey-bang up his daisy,
The likes I never saw before.

She wore a bonnet on her pate,
Was given by her granny Kate.
Made out of the skin of a buck-goat,
To get his skin they cut his throat.
This bonnet was adorned with feathers

From a guinea-hen,
Which made them both look fresh and fair,
When mounted on their chestnut mare.

Her shape and make I will tell you.
She was big-eyed and pug-nosed too;
Lantern-jawed, herring-gutted,
Lobster-backed, besides web-footed;
She was bow-legged and knock-kneed,
She was a beauty, they all agreed.
She was a promise, they all cursed.
As Satan said when dry-nursed
The monkey on his sooty knee
The devil's nurse I'm sure was he.

So now to you the truth I'll tell,
This daughter he did portion well.
She got a pig, a tub, a cow,
A trencher, ladles and a pan,
Besides a goose and a gander got
A turkey for the pot,
The pride of all her granny's flock.

Of flaxen stow she got three stone,
I believe for money she got none.
Of asses she got ninety four
And the promise of another score.

And to the wedding they did return
And a hungry weaver there did mourn.
Pat demanded silence in the place,
Till he would hear the weaver's case.
And he began without a lie
I thought he would set up a cry.
His teeth did fail him he confessed
Before them all without a jest,
And before that, half his fill he ate,
The place was fairly cleared of mate.
Pat hung a cord in the hall

Which rung a bell on the jamb wall.
The greasy cook came waddling in,
Saying master what makes all the din.
This greedy weaver's hungry still
Curse on his gut, give him his fill.

The cook brought in a dish of kale,
Well dressed with oil and barley male,
Salad, sorrel, kitchen stuff,
Fishes guts and leeks enough.
The greedy weaver ate so fast
That he was near being choked at last,
But a watchful barber standing by,
He on the weaver cast an eye;
He straight away pulled from his throat
The lights and livers of a goat,
Besides ten or eleven foot
Of potato pudding and fish gut,
Who says he, and his children all,
Who prostrate on their knees should pray
For his good fortune night and day.

The late Paddy Cassidy (of the Irish Kitchen Museum in the Corner House Bar, Lisnaskea) had this poem in his collection back in the 1970's. I transcribed it exactly as I saw it then. Apparently, this was a very well known 'spat' over a wide area for a long time. But it seems that it has now fallen into obscurity - even around Roslea.

The degree of exaggeration in this rhyme places it in the realm of fantasy but there is, nevertheless, an intriguing range of occupations and food mentioned. You wonder if it was inspired by a real wedding or if 'Pat' is of the proverbial kind. The prevalence of sea-food 'lobsters, oysters, mussels, cockles' in such a land-locked place as Roslea (in 1819!) is strange. Bird lovers will be appalled by the 'fowl' plates of 'crane, and plovers, larks and snipes.' The fairer sex will be bemused by the author's idea of 'beauty' - 'lantern-jawed, lobster-backed' though perhaps the day will return when they will be glad to receive as a marriage inducement 'a pig, a tub, a cow.' But we can only wonder at what the good woman would have done with ninety four asses and 'the promise of another score.' You also wonder if the author had a thing about weavers. Were weavers seen as 'greedy' at that time? Maybe we should steer well clear of such 'reading into' the text; it might raise more questions than it would answer.

Pictures of the Past
by Sean McElgunn

One Sunday, in the early summer of 1936, Dad borrowed Uncle Pat Grogan's horse and trap, and we went visiting. We jogged out the newly tarred Clones Road at a merry trot. It was wonderful to see the sun shining on the golden thatch and whitewashed walls of the houses we passed. After a while Dad pulled on the reins and said wo-o-o! to the horse. This is the Border, he said; the horse is in the Wee Six and we are still in the Free State. I could see nothing. Dad made a clicking sound with his tongue and we jogged on, across Wattlebridge and on down to Lanbrock Cross, where Aunt Maggy and Uncle Mick lived in a lovely thatched house. They had no children but they had a shop. The gander stuck out his neck and chased me with a fierce hiss. My younger brother found a stick and chased the gander. We all got sweets in the shop although it was closed on the outside because it was Sunday. That was a magic day, my first time in Fermanagh. When it came time to leave, my older sister was invited to stay for the whole summer holidays. To make it up to me and my mournful face, it was agreed that I could come for the Christmas holidays.

It took Stephen's Day a lifetime to arrive. Dad put me up in front of him on the Charleyhorse's back, and we jogged out to Granda's. I waited another age for Francie the cotsman. Lizzy was Granda's housekeeper and Francie's sister; they came from across the Border in Fermanagh. At long last I spotted the tiny figure coming over the distant hill; as I watched his whistling came drifting on a gust of wind. But Francie had to get tea and bring all the news from home. And I kept making faces over the half-door (The Rocks o'Bawn). More waiting for the latest news from home and of course tea, and I stomped around outside and made faces across the half-door. We walked the two miles to Quivvy Lodge and Francie pulled down the Lough. My very first time on the water had me spellbound up in the prow. This was a totally different world, the land sliding backwards, the swans and baldies and waterhens moving slowly out of our way, all the time keeping a beady eye on us. The Lough had me in thrall forever. We landed at Derradoon Quay and walked two more miles to Lambrock Cross, where Aunty lived. I was so tired that I must have fallen asleep.

Waking to the musical sing-song voices wafting up from the shop below, where was I? I had slept with Dan, the servant-boy. I stared up at the baggy, whitewashed sacking above, with the bedposts going up through, then down the steep ladder in my nightshirt, I was sent back to bed with a buttered currant biscuit as big as a plate. We went to Mass on New Year's morning to Newtown in the horse-and-trap, and the priest scoulded us through two long sermons. Then off to Uncle Mick's Aunt Rose's Hotel and Master McCormack's. Then home for Bridgie's dinner of goose and more plum-pudding. Bridgie was the servant-girl.

They had a magic box called a wireless in the kitchen. I can hear Barney McCool from Coolaghy singing 'Tyrone among the bushes'; I can see it all right now, the soft light of the Tilley-lamp, the Chinamen on the big blue dishes, the goldfish sleeping with her head under her wing. This would last forever, like Heaven.

Glossary
Baldies = Coots

40

When London Trees Let Down Their Leaves
by Tony Brady

Roland was regarded as a fantasist by the other homeless men living with him at the hostel called Launcelot Andrewes House, Southwark. They did not believe his stories about his exploits in the Special Armed Services. I knew better having accessed his background thoroughly. When Roland moved into his council flat in Shoreditch he posted the SAS logo *"Who Dares Wins!"* on his front door and was not pleased when I, involved with him as his re-settlement support worker, suggested this was unwise; it was a time when IRA bombs were going off in London. Roland was a re-settlement success despite the periodic absences from his flat.

He would leave me signs that he was away such as a matchstick inserted between his front door and the frame or a tiny patch of cellotape over the Yale lock keyhole of his flat. He showed me how to leave a message, when he was not at home, in the form of a paper javelin blown through his letter box with just enough force to land on a spot that was visible when I peeped through. If it was still there on my next visiting call and I got no reply to my knock I would know Roland was still away.

Roland told me that, as an ex-SAS man, he must always be ready for an instant recall so he had to keep himself in full readiness. Oftentimes, he would de-camp to Dartmoor, in Devon and The New Forest, in Hampshire or to other remote places and live rough to keep himself in trim. A few nights in a London park was all part of the necessary exercises. A year after we agreed that he required no further support I took a call from his local housing officer who said that Roland had been missing for over six months and his flat was re-possessed. More months passed: then the Coroner's Officer at Highbury, Islington asked me to come to the mortuary and identify a body that had been found in undergrowth in Finsbury Park; it was the mortal remains of Roland.

I went to the Inquest as the only person known to Roland as he had specified me as a friend in notes found on his body: they were carefully swaddled in plastic together with his name, rank, number etc. The verdict was natural causes. Police speculated that Roland was sheltering in undergrowth and died of a heart attack - as there were no injuries to his body. Commuters on the top deck of their regular bus had alerted the park authority: they had noticed the body gradually appearing over a number of days as winds blew aside the leaves that had fallen and covered it. A sad story: but now somehow, Roland (though unidentified) in the poem *Autumn Revelation* is immortalized.

Autumn Revelation
by Tony Brady

The fallen leaves that spun in leaps
and bounds at every chattering gust
now lie trapped in rustling heaps
or whirl about as drifting dust

An Haiku
by Tony Brady

Retirement. Time, being of
less importance,
colleagues present you
with a watch.

The End of an Era....
by Tony Brady

"It's The End of an Era!" - said Albert to Dolly,
People's shares are gone and so's their lolly!
"How can that be?" said Dolly to Bert -
"We're flush and you've still got your shirt!

People borrowed beyond their means - My Dear -
all that is left now is a climate of fear.
But don't turn a hair, Dolly - worry no more!
All our investments are safely off-shore!

It's the end of an era Dolly! Make the lunch
while I fill you in on the Credit Crunch.
Sub-Prime credit, that's what caused The Crash
And now the Banks are strapped for cash.

No chance for a mortgage, or even a loan,
"The End of an Era" is the general moan.
Where's all the profits? Surely the onus
must rest on the greedy cult of the bonus.

Seemingly, not a single person's to blame
as nobody knows the rules of the game.
Still, Praise the Lord! To thee much thanks!
The Government has bought the Banks.

The End of an Era! Still it marks a new start
for clever schemes that will help you part
with your hard earned money, unless instead
you take my advice to keep it under your bed.

Whatever happens - we can't at last relax
as we all have to pay - my dearest Dolly -
for the folly of those who lost the lolly
with a bigger burden of personal tax.

The Funeral of Jemmy Leonard
by Frank McHugh

Gerry turned to his daughter, Maggie, and gestured her upstairs. Managing to get a seat in the gallery, with the front of the church empty, they waited for the family mourners to arrive. It is clear that there are not enough seats for those who have accompanied the family cortege. It is a big funeral. Many of the extended family end up standing outside the church, while locals sit in comfort. Gerry spots a big man waiting by the organ in the gallery and initially mistakes him for Paddy Leonard, Jemmy's eldest son, long since moved away. At the start of the funeral mass, the big man starts to sing with a beautiful tenor voice, and Gerry realises it can't be Paddy's melodious bass tone. He is clearly a performer, used to the public stage, brought in to give the funeral an air of formality and status. There is an aura about the big man's presence and the church fills with his rendition of 'How Great thou Art', Gerry's favourite hymn. He can remember sitting in his bedroom in the little bungalow he shared with his grandmother, listening to the gospel sounds of Dolly Parton. The funeral has the feel of local royalty and the opening song, with the big man in full flow, seems to emphasise this. There is a final delay, before the funeral begins, as they wait for Jemmy's wife, Sally to be seated in the sacristy.

So this is local royalty. As Gerry's mother liked to remind him, Tommy Leonard, Jemmy's father was once a servant to his great-grandfather, Paddy Greene. But now the tables are turned. The Leonards have moved up in the world, owners of real estate all over the country. After Father Jones' homily, Paddy Leonard walks to the pulpit and momentarily is overtaken with emotion as he looks out at the congregation. He starts to talk about his father and conveys that sense of awe that most men feel about their fathers. The sense of learning from the father and how the cycle of life turns the tables and the master regresses back to childhood. In his speech Paddy acknowledges the hard upbringing endured by his father and Gerry feels embarrassed by his earlier thoughts. Paddy reveals that Jemmy's father died when he was 11. So like Gerry's grandfather, he spent most of his life without his father.

The Funeral Mass continued with the usual formalities. At the end of the service, Father Jones agreed to people expressing their condolences inside the church, which meant that Sally didn't have to endure the cold harsh weather by the graveside. Following the death of Tommy Hoy, it is clear that the old generation are passing on. Gerry senses that his Great Uncle's turn will come soon. There aren't many of his age left. As Jemmy's coffin descends into the grave, Gerry remembers his father. Families are all the same in death. The trappings may be different. But the journey remains.

The Drainage on the Upper Erne
Composed by John Foynes, Butlersbridge,
air The Gentle Maiden, Collected by Sean McElgunn

As I sit all alone by the watchfire, awaiting the morning to dawn
I think of the time that has passed since the drainage it first here began
It started I think in harvest in the year of Our Lord '34
There was work, there was laughing and singing, the likes as never heard before

There were men here from round Bellaconnell, Derralin and Milltown and Redhills
Some working with picks and with shovels, some with compressors and drills
The engineers, gangers and crewmen, from north, south, east, west, they came all
Our foreman, he trated us dacent, was Butler from oul Donegal

Back then the great wheels of industry were turning on axles so swift
From the dole and free-beef at McKernans' employment it came as a gift
Two men met their fate in Belturbet, they married two damsels in town
Not a lass would be left for the locals, that was the story went round

They built a big boat at Belturbet, with a dredger well out to the fore
To scour up the Erne's wide waters that couldn't be reached from the shore
The names of the places she sailed to, I'll mention tonight if I can
She sailed up to lovely Lough Oughter, and halted a while there at Rann

Killakeen was the next port of calling, an inlet she there did enlarge
And she sailed to a place called the Derries, her duty up there to discharge
She started the journey back homeward but a storm arose on the way
And she sank in the wild, roaring surges at the mouth of Cloghoughter's broad bay

Christmas she spent neath the waters awaiting the dawning New Year
She was raised once again from her slumbers and back to her base she did steer
Big Charley was one of the horses that worked twice as hard as the man
Who went weak at the sight of a shovel and never came back again

No more at the end of each fortnight Black Pat with his bag will go round
Content we must be at McKernans' till other employment is found
Goodbye to my friends and companions, the captain and crew of the boat
Some day we may sail her again boys if ev'r she chances to float.

Glossary - Free beef = vouchers for free beef given to the unemployed in Ireland in the 1930s and early 1990s.

Some Reflections on the Erne Hydroelectricity Scheme
by Michael Donnelly

The success of the Shannon Hydro Electricity scheme which opened in 1929 immediately led to consideration of a similar operation on the Erne. When a young engineer first mooted the Shannon scheme it was generally considered impractical in the case of a river which could scarcely get itself out of the country. The Erne posed the problem of the catchment area falling outside of the Irish Free State. Ideally the proper management of the scheme would involve accommodation works in the Northern jurisdiction and agreements on the control of flow and water levels, which in the perceived climate of political relations must have seemed unlikely. The fact that both sides of the border stood to benefit was the engine that drove the scheme to fruition and the processes involved have exercised commentators and journalists to a notable degree. The actual operation of the work has also produced a number of treatises of interest to the engineering and construction specialists. The social aspect is largely ignored. Earlier schemes of drainage within a single jurisdiction had encountered a share of opposition, perhaps because the affected interests were of a different order, and in today's social climate they would be much more fraught. Doubtless environmental concerns as well as physical ones were examined but there were no environmental impact assessments to be prepared for planning consent, no Friends of the Earth or green lobbies in the field, and much less active legal examination to contend with. Wartime conditions had made for a more docile and accepting public. Those affected remained disconnected individuals almost like casualties of the war effort. There was a considerable loss of habitat, business and way of life, and loss of life itself in some cases. I propose to take a look at some of those features as recorded or spoken of but a brief outline of the scheme is first desirable.

The river Erne is approximately 60 miles from its source at Lough Gowna in Cavan to the sea below Ballyshannon in Donegal. Two major lakes, Upper and Lower Erne are in Northern Ireland, the maximum levels of these before development were 158.00, and 155.00 DD. There was about 2.0 ft. fall from Enniskillen to Belleek 22 miles distant and 143 ft. from that to upper sea levels 9 miles distant. The average discharge at Belleek was 3350 cusecs (cubic feet, per second) annually but flood rate rose to 11,000 cusecs. There were control sluices at Belleek since 1890 and all in good order but with the problem that the flow exceeded the input here in drought periods. Steep drops at Cliff, below Belleek and at Ballyshannon determined the location of the generators and the Ballyshannon drop was maximized by damming the river at Cathleen Falls and forming a lake, Assaroe Lake behind it. This involved rerouting parts of the roads from Belleek and raising a levee at a section where the road and adjoining land is below the reservoir water level. Most of the land on this, the south side was in the Camlin estate, much of which had been acquired some years previously by the Land Commission. The remaining 449 acres, including the castle, was on the market and was purchased in the same manner in 1948. Several miles

The Erne Hydro-Electric Stations, Ballyshannon (top image) and Cliff Station, Belleek.

of riparian land extending from the dam to the Camlin estate belonged to Richard Cassidy whose house and farm buildings lay close to the dam on a narrow section of land between the road and the river. He refused to co-operate with the land acquisition service, but this was nonetheless effected including requisitioning of a substantial part of the farmhouse outbuildings. He remained in residence throughout the duration of the works which included extensive rock blasting nearby. The windows on the river side of the house particularly suffered and eventually were protected from flying debris. The story of his resistance was enacted in a radio drama, "Farewell to every white cascade," written by his grandson Frank Harvey and entered by Radio Eireann for the international Italia prize.

The North bank had a more fractured ownership of small holdings, including the original Cassidy homestead, and the imposing Laputa house. Land rose gradually from the river on this side. The minor road on this side was less affected but all the land south of the road is now submerged, including dwellings, farm buildings, a mill and granary and a small church. There was no organized resistance to the requisition from the owners including among them, my father who received approximately £330 for a small farm of 15 acres. Camlin Castle was expected to be submerged also but remains in ruined condition on dry land. This seems to be a remarkable miscalculation. The forestry trees were offered for sale at £200 but the short time span worked against this opportunity. The imposing tower gateway still flanks the road. No Tredennick ownership interest exists here now and presumably the gate avenue and rains are in public ownership with little sign of management. The station at Cliff did away with Cliff House, the seat of the Connolly family, and some lesser big houses were also lost.

The contract for the two power stations and the restructuring of the Erne with the necessary ancillary works was awarded to an English engineering company from Doncaster, the Cementation Company, who also subsequently negotiated the contract for the drainage scheme and control gates in the Northern State. Deaths occurred during this operation. In both operations a labour camp was formed, housed in Nissan type huts in one case and in timber buildings for the works upstream, where relatively few of the workers were domiciled sufficiently close to the sites. In Ballyshannon there was a high involvement of specialist skills and products and these were frequently sourced abroad, in England, in Germany where the turbines were supplied from, and Sweden where much of the electrical equipment for transmission and transformers was sourced. A culture of hard drinking is rampant in labour camps. Many of the locals considered themselves to be world class in this capacity but the big men from the Northern lands were more than equal to the locals in the home pubs, which seems surprising in view of the prohibition culture then existing in Sweden. The Sweden factor also came into focus in a tragic attempt at sabotage in later years.

The rocky river channel from the dam to the bridge was heavily remodelled involving rock excavation and blasting. Cementation used limestone from this to manufacture the cement required for much or perhaps all the material required for the dam and turbine housing, a huge and commendable economy of means. Among the casualties of these works was a huge rock exposed at ebb tide on which the incoming salmon could be seen utilizing it to rid themselves of sea lice.

The following is an extract from Frank Harvey's "Farewell to every white cascade":
Excerpts from the play are reproduced by kind permission of the author.

TERENCE: (SUDDENLY, IN AN EXCITED VOICE). Granda! Granda! I think there's going to be a blast! There's a man waving a red flag over on the far road, and stopping all the cars.

RICHARD: (HALF SUNK IN REVERIE). A blast . . .a blast. . .noise. . .noise. . .more noise. . .(THEN AS HE SLOWLY REALISES THE IMPLICATION OF TERENCE'S WORDS). You'd better come back from the window, boy, and sit down here by the bed. It'll be safer.

TERENCE: I wonder will it be a big one?

RICHARD: I suppose it'll be like all the rest, a great big bang. But anyway you'd be better to come over here till it's over.

(SOUND OF MOVEMENT AS TERENCE LEAVES WINDOW AND SITS BY BED)

TERENCE: Listen, Granda! The river! Can you hear it? All the machines have stopped.

(COMPLETE SILENCE EXCEPT FOR THE DISTANT SOUND OF THE RIVER PLUNGING OVER THE FALLS)

RICHARD: Yes, I can hear it, the same old sound of the water like it always used to be. But everything's very quiet all of a sudden even with the window shut. Listen, there's a blackbird started to sing down in the planting.

(SOUND OF A BLACKBIRD SINGING IN THE DISTANCE)

TERENCE: There's hardly a sound except the river and the blackbird.

RICHARD: So - like the strange quiet before the thunderclap. I think. . .

TERENCE: The blast!

(SOUND OF A DEAFENING EXPLOSION THAT SHAKES THE WHOLE HOUSE. SOUND OF TINKLING CRASH OF BROKEN GLASS AS WINDOW IS BURST IN. THEN A GREAT SPLINTERING CRASH AS A HUGE BOULDER TEARS THROUGH THE CEILING AND BURIES ITSELF IN THE FLOOR BESIDE THE BED)

TERENCE: (ALMOST IN TEARS). Oh Granda! Granda! We'll all be killed! Look at the size of the stone in the floor!

RICHARD: (HIS VOICE A LITTLE TREMULOUS). Hold my hand, son, and sit where you are. It's all over now, thank God. It was a bad one, all right.

(SOUND OF APPROACHING FOOTSTEPS AND VOICES)

KATIE: (OFF MIKE). Are you all right? Are you all right?

JOHN: (OFF MIKE). Terence! Father! Are you hurt?

KATIE: (OFF MIKE). Glory be to God, John, will you look at the size of the rock in the floor!

JOHN:	(OFF MIKE). Are you all right, Terence? Father? I can't see right with all the dust.
RICHARD:	Aye, we're all right, thanks be to God. But the rock just missed the bed. Somebody was praying for us.
KATIE:	Ah, the poor child! Are you all right, Terence?
TERENCE:	(SNIFFLING). I'm all right now, Mammy, but I was frightened.
JOHN:	Good God! Look at the window! There's hardly a bit of glass left in it. They said this was the last big blast and I hope to God it is.

(A BRIEF SILENCE)

TERENCE:	(SUDDENLY BREAKING OUT INTO LOUD SOBBING CRIES). Listen! Oh, listen! Oh, Granda, listen! The river! The sound of the river is gone! Oh, Granda, they've blasted away the falls forever! The river! The river!
KATIE:	There now, Terence! There now, the poor child! Come on down with me. That's a good boy.

(SOUND OF RECEDING FOOTSTEPS AND SOBBING)

JOHN:	Are you sure you're all right, Father?

(SILENCE)

JOHN:	(ANXIOUSLY REPEATING THE PHRASE). Father, are you all right?
RICHARD:	(MUSING, IN A LOW HOARSE TREMULOUS VOICE). The river. . .the river. . . the sound of the river is gone. . .gone forever. . .(HE BEGINS TO RECITE IN A LOW VOICE CHARGED WITH EMOTION THE SIXTH STANZA OF WILLIAM ALLINGHAM'S "Adieu to Ballyshannon")
RICHARD:	(RECITING). "Farewell to every white cascade, from the Harbour to Belleek, And every pool where fins may rest, and ivy-shaded creek, The sloping fields, the lofty rocks, where ash and holly grow; The one split yew tree gazing on the curving flood below; The lough that winds. . .

(FADE GRADUALLY)

The above would seem to indicate a rather cavalier approach to the operational hazards by the contractors. There were safety regulations but the biggest factor in employer concern could have been insurance. Self responsibility was much greater then in determining compensation costs. This has shifted almost entirely to the employer side and with greater regulation and enforcement the thirteen deaths in course of the works would seem inconceivable now. These included several falls, machine accidents and a workshop electrocution. Casualties were not limited to basic workers, and there were many non fatal events. The labour camp operation with its similarity to military style would and will always be fraught. It is surprising that contractors' site buildings would have been sited in a danger zone. They may have been better protected and evacuated on critical occasions. The main structures were formed behind the dams and housed the turbines, 2 No. turbo alternator sets at Ballyshannon, with output of 22.5 MW on 95 ft (29m) head, and two at Cliff, output 10 MW on 40 ft.(l0m) head, and a small generator of 300 W for operational purposes as well as control rooms for the works, now largely obsolete, as the system is now fully automated with a skeleton staff of six in Ballyshannon and no operational staff at all at Cliff. The original control room is retained with all its dials and controls as an exhibition feature. Initially staff numbers, which were probably generous, amounted to 122. The reduction in staff presently 29 has been to some extent utilized for new uses such as occasional public sight seeing tours, and the approach remains as, formerly, off the Belleek road.

The transmission equipment site adjoins the generator site just above the entrance to the works. This was the scene of the death of a man from Northern Ireland who was involved in an unsuccessful attempt at industrial sabotage. He was an employee of the Northern Ireland Electricity Board's outdoor staff. The two electricity boards had harmonious working relations but this didn't extend to all staff. As it happened, the equipment of Swedish manufacture was unfamiliar and resulted in the attacker suffering severe burns, compounded by the trip switch being reopened three times before the problem was recognized. The man was taken to the nearby Sheil Hospital where he died a day later. Apparently he had a girlfriend in the support group who had to be dragged to the escape car. Security provisions were put in place at both stations, which, however resulted only in the apprehension of two local poachers at Cliff, who were not detained long.

The other populations affected adversely by the development were likely to be the migratory fish, salmon and eel. A stepped by-pass is provided for salmon and a count of numbers moving up river is kept. The figures from the ESB show that the estimated number of fish moving upriver prior to the operation had actually increased six years after the opening. The outward journey of the young smolts and mature eels is not recordable but they must necessarily pass through the turbines and apparently in the case of the much larger eels, only occasionally is there evidence left behind of this occurring. Some accounts would have it that slaughter is widespread. However some 4,000,000 elvers are now trapped annually in a holding pond and transported by road for placement in the catchment area and also in Lough Neagh. Commercial eel fishing is no longer permitted but the decline in salmon is general and has many other causes and conjectured causes. These include fishing, both commercial, legal and illegal, and UDN disease, still a mystery, but not at present a problem, and measures taken to address the decline in stocks have apparently helped. These have involved a ban on offshore and estuary netting and the establishment of a hatchery at Ballyshannon.

However the comparative catching rates in the nearby Drowes river would suggest some measure of responsibility is due to the scheme. Salmon are caught in the Drowes starting New Years Day but traditionally none appeared in the Erne before June.

The dam at Ballyshannon was designed to cope with an exceptional risk event, calculated to occur once in a century and a greater risk event which would have a thousand year cycle. This would involve severe flood conditions in the catchment area and exceptional tide and storm conditions in the estuary. The new bridge would be most at risk. Since inception an event nearing the design limit was experienced but whether this was the 100 year or the 1000 year extreme is uncertain. In 1970 the world was apparently awash with oil and prices low and falling. The ESB started to speak of the plant being at the limit of its economic life and no longer a viable option for replacement. This quickly changed with the Middle Eastern crisis and there was no further mention of decommissioning or costly replacement. Recently a costly replacement event occurred, due to the major part now requiring a made to order procedure with limited contracting options available. However hydroelectricity remains the cheapest source. This may change in the future and some major adjustments would be necessary. The output of 32.5 MW was 6% of the total generated by the electricity service initially but now amounts to approximately 2%.

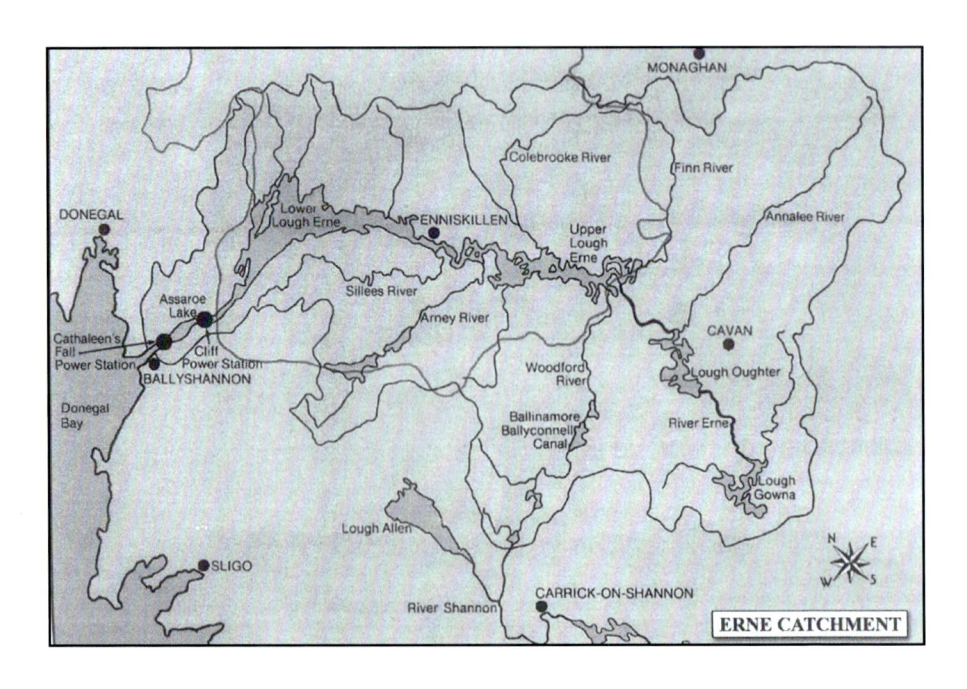

Wellington, the Iron Duke and a bit of an Enigma
by Vicky Herbert

We often hear about Wellington through the television series 'Sharpe' which dwells on his fearless tactics in battles against Napoleon in the Peninsular War. Every time we put on a pair of wellies we should think of him because his riding boots were of such style that they became synonymous with his name. The full name for them is 'Wellington Boots'!

In Enniskillen we know about him from his association with our local Royal Inniskilling Fusiliers and the Inniskilling Dragoons. Both regiments fought at Waterloo and distinguished themselves so well that Napoleon is supposed to have asked, who are the soldiers with the castle on their caps, and when told that they were the Inniskillings, commented that 'they do not know when they are beaten!' One historian wrote about the Dragoons that 'Never in the annals of modern warfare was a cavalry charge more decisive.' And Wellington added 'they saved the centre of my line at Waterloo.' One estimate is that one third of Wellington's soldiers were Irish.

We also have another connection with Wellington and Napoleon in Fermanagh due to the economic upsurge because of the war. As a result of the Napoleonic wars the linen trade flourished and weavers were in demand for the cloth to make the uniforms. Farmers were also kept busy producing food for the armies. So up to 1815 there was a great prosperity in Fermanagh. There were also forts built in Enniskillen at that time, the Star Fort at Fort Hill to the east, and the Redoubt by the West Bridge. An invasion by Napoleonic forces was expected, and people came inland even from the Sligo area to escape the French fleet as they had done in 1798 when they came as far as the West Bridge but were not allowed into the town in case they overcrowded it so had to camp there. The Street was called 'Beggars Street' before it was renamed 'Henry Street', because of this influx and the previous one.

The Star Fort, Forthill - now the site of the Cole Memorial

Napoleonic Redoubt, West Bridge

So what is the Wellington enigma? I had known that he was Irish but had said some rather strange things about his place of birth, which was, I thought, unusual in itself. Most people look back nostalgically to their origins. He had been quoted as saying 'Just because you are born in a stable, it doesn't mean that you are a horse' which could either mean that he looked down on his place of birth or he was comparing himself with the other very famous person who was actually born in a stable!

Which was true? He was being taunted about his country of origin in Parliament when he supposedly made this remark, And then, what was it that made people so cross at him that they actually renamed places, which had been called after him at the height of his military triumph? For example, behind the Bank of Ireland in Darling Street, Enniskillen, there was an area called Wellington Place. It had started life as Wellington Street in 1800 (it was home to some local merchants and two Wesleyan ministers), and is marked on a map, dated 1833 in the Museum as such. Then it had been changed to Eldon Place when Wellington was out of favour in Enniskillen on account of his support for Catholic Emancipation (Lord Eldon was renowned for his zeal against Catholics) and this was marked on another map in the Museum dated 1842. But people could not get used to the new name and always called it Wellington Street anyway! But it was again called after the national hero when a few years had passed and the map dated 1858 in the museum called it Wellington Place again! Why was this? I love a historic mystery and I did a bit of delving.

So I was intrigued when a friend lent me a book to read that her mother had collected a long time ago. It was called 'The Dublin University Magazine' no. CIX vol. XIX and was dated January 1842. I like genuinely old books, even the smell of them is tantalising, but it's a bit scary turning pages that you think might break or fall out at any time! So at first I thought that I would have a brief flick through, maybe read just the article about the Corn Laws (we had been working on the history of Workhouses in Ireland and the Great Famine of 1845) and give the volume back to Diana. But then I saw the articles about Wellington, and they linked in with two other books (modern I hasten to add) I had just read, one about Sharpe set in 1813 and the other about troops going to

South Africa, set in 1827. Both of them had mentioned Wellington, but had made me wonder why he was so opposed to some of the legislation back then. The article in the 1842 book was called 'Maxwell's Life of Wellington' and discussed an earlier 1839 book. These are some of the facts gleaned from that.

Wellington was born in 1769 (the same year, funnily enough, that Napoleon was born!) and he was the fourth son of the Earl of Mornington who seemed to be a very pleasant gentleman, and who had started a loan fund, composed several pieces of music and altogether not the man we would have expected the Iron Duke to spring from. Wellington, whose family name was Wellesley, went to Eton then to a military college in Angiers, France. He came back to Trim where he stood for the Irish Parliament and made speeches about the penal code and the enfranchisement of Catholics, which were well received locally. He also got into debt and his landlord at the time, Mr. Dixon, helped him by lending him money, which Wellington repaid as soon as he could. That in itself was a bit of an eye opener to me! And maybe it was a lesson he never forgot.

He got his first commission in 1787 and in 1792 was put in charge of the 18th Light Dragoons. His rise up the martial ladder was very quick indeed, probably by reason of his aristocracy, and by September 1793 he had been made a Lieutenant-Colonel. That must have annoyed the veterans over whose heads he was promoted. It was indeed fortunate that Wellington had the talent for command, unlike the later military disasters of the Crimean War and the Charge of the Light Brigade. His first active service was under the command of Lord Moira who took reinforcements out to the Duke of York, Frederick, who was in retreat from the French in the Netherlands. Lord Moira returned to England but Wellington remained and was instrumental in saving the lives of many soldiers who would otherwise have been obliterated by the attacking French. The Duke of York was recalled to England. This was the Duke about whom the children's chant was composed:-

> The Grand Old Duke of York, he had 10,000 men,
> He marched them up to the top of the hill,
> Then he marched them down again
> And when they were up, they were up
> And when they were down, they were down
> And when they were only half way up
> They were neither up nor down!

His next military assignment was in India where his brother, now Lord Mornington, had been appointed Governor-General. An attack was mounted on the Sultan of Mysore who had formed a confederacy against the Crown and after the taking of his capital, Wellington was put in charge of the city, over the head of more experienced soldiers. This was obviously an act of favouritism, but Wellington proved equal to the task and continued to show his skills in various battles in India.

When Wellington (Sir Arthur) returned from India he married the third daughter of Lord Longford and a year after his marriage he accepted the office of Chief Secretary of Ireland in 1807. He served under what was called 'a strong government' and passed acts, which matched that government

Then Wellington was redeployed to the Peninsular Wars and sailed from Cork to Spain on the 12th July 1808, in his ship 'The Crocodile'. He was to serve under Sir Hew Dalrymple and Sir Harry Burrard, not command the army himself. He returned to Ireland and took up his office of Chief Secretary again, until he was sent back to the Peninsula, this time as supreme commander and fought many successful battles against the French generals. Did Wellington earn his title of 'the Iron Duke' from these battles? He seemed to have his eyes everywhere and was able to send reinforcements or to mount charges where needed, despite not having much support from other generals and armies. Was this why he was called 'The Iron Duke'?

No, the title of 'The Iron Duke' did not actually come from his war prowess, or his strict regime, although it is tempting to believe so. Well then, did it come from his character? He often appeared condescending in public, never spoke to servants if he could help it and showed no emotion at all. When informed by a blackmailing publisher that a former mistress threatened to name Wellington in her memoirs, it was Wellington who said 'publish and be damned'. So not a man you could take lightly or draw close to, then. But his steely character still isn't the answer.

It was his opposition to 'the Reform Act' of 1830, which turned some people against him. It is strange that he opposed that, because he was in complete favour previously of Catholic emancipation and gave his best speech in the House of Lords, facing stiff opposition and showing that he felt for the people where he was born and understood their grievances. The Catholic Relief Act of 1829 was passed by a majority of 105, pushed through only with the help of the Whigs, with many Tories voting against the Act (Wellington was a Tory). But the 'Reform Act' was another kettle of fish. Wellington did not agree with it and opposed it despite the riots (called 'the swing riots') in London in 1830 to have it passed. He erected iron shutters on the windows of his residence in London, Apsley House, to prevent the windows being broken by stones thrown by the pro-reformers. This was the reason for his title 'The Iron Duke'. Not his character or his steadfastness in battle.

Wellington lost the vote of confidence on 15th November 1830 and was replaced by Earl Grey. The Reform Bill was passed in 1832 after a lot of political jostling and actually was desperately needed. Before 1832, only one adult male in ten had the right to vote. The Reform Act doubled this and it did away with most of the 'rotten' or 'pocket' boroughs, such as Old Sarum which had only seven voters, all controlled by the local squire, but sent two members to parliament. It reapportioned members of parliament but also gave power of voting to lower and middle classes, extending franchise to any man owning a house worth £10. It achieved in England what Revolution did in France, but without the guillotine. However, landed gentry, like Wellington, didn't think that 'ordinary people' knew enough to make big decisions, presumably. We have learnt over the years that this thinking was wrong. Well, that's why he was called 'The Iron Duke'. Was that why the place name was changed in Enniskillen?

The Duke of Wellington

In fact, that was actually because he voted for Catholic Emancipation. Trimble, in volume 3 of his History of Enniskillen said that the Corporation in Enniskillen who were mostly Tories were against the Catholic Emancipation Act so did not support Wellington. They renamed the street 'Eldon Row' after Lord Eldon, the man in parliament who was the chief opponent of the Act. So Wellington was censured for supporting the one act and opposing the other! However, I don't think it affected him much, do you? He was obviously a man who did not mind a bit of controversy!

And Now Let's Hear It For The Duck
by John Cunningham

Having trodden the boards over many years, from amateur dramatics to musicals and following in the steps of my father who did likewise in the 1940s and 1950s, I thought I might record some of my theatrical memoirs now that I have a son and daughter falling into similar thespian ways. I grew up in the '50s faithfully attending St. Joseph's Hall, Ederney, where, during the winter months a succession of plays and concert parties performed, invariably for local Parochial Funds. It was the norm at the time that each parish organised a play and after local performances took it on tour to neighbouring parishes and in particular those who had brought their play to Ederney Hall. The ultimate producer was invariably the Parish Priest or Curate who cajoled or inveigled a number of the local teachers to take part and then left them to get on with it. In the days before television there were only radio programmes to while away the long winter nights so it was a bit of fun and diversion to attend rehearsals and pack into a few cars to visit surrounding areas on frosty nights to do our thing for parish funds. Props had to be kept to a minimum and swift reordering of entrances and exits was normal on a strange stage. The curtain might or might not open, or close to order, bulbs of the footlights might fuse but it was all part of the hazards to be negotiated around. Your play might need three entry points but had to make do with two or even one if that was all that was there. Learning to adjust to an unfamiliar stage and carry on the performance as best one could was a prerequisite of the actor and actresses. There was no room for prima donnas.

Probably the most popular of the plays selected were of the genre of Irish rural/kitchen comedies e.g. George Shiels (24 June 1881 - 19 September 1949) an Irish dramatist whose plays were a success both in his native Ulster and at the Abbey Theatre in Dublin. His most famous plays are *The Rugged Path*, *The Passing Day*, and *The New Gossoon*. Shiels was born in Ballymoney, County Antrim, and emigrated to Canada as a young man. While working on the building of the Canadian Pacific Railway in 1913, he was involved in a serious accident that left him in a wheelchair for the rest of his life. He returned to Ballymoney and started a shipping company with his brother, and also began writing at this time. Starting with poems and short stories, he soon progressed to plays, which he provided to the Ulster Literary Theatre under the pen name of *George S. Morsheils*. Starting with *Bedmates* (1921), his plays began to be regularly accepted by the Abbey Theatre for production. His 1930 work *The New Gossoon* was so well-received that the Abbey's touring company, The Abbey Theatre Irish Players, brought the play to Broadway for limited runs three times, in 1932, 1934, and 1937. In 1940, a production of Shiels' *The Rugged Path* set an Abbey record by attracting a total audience of 25,000 people over eight weeks.

When his success as a playwright allowed him, he left the shipping business and moved to Carnlough on the coast of County Antrim, where he lived from 1932 until his death in 1949. Of his thirty plays, in addition to those mentioned above I would have seen in my childhood, *Moodie in Manitoba* (1918), *Paul Twyning* (1922), *Professor*

Tim (1925), *Neal Maquade* (1938) - later revised as *Macook's Corner* (1942) and *Give Him a House* (1939). Thomas King Moylan, 1885-1958 was another favourite playwright. He was clerk of Grangegorman Mental Hospital who wrote comedy plays, including *Paid in his Own Coin; Tactics; Naboclish; Uncle Pat* (1913); *The Curse of the Country* (1917); *Movies* and *Lawsy Me* (1918); and *A Damsel from Dublin* (1945). These were very popular with amateur dramatic companies. The audiences did not set high theatrical standards but they expected to be entertained and that's what we had to deliver.

Mind you, we did have a degree of competition and this took the form of the Travelling Shows who visited the local towns and set up for a week or fortnight in a local hall with some pitching a large tent in a field adjoining. These included Courtney Brothers who frequented Pettigo and the Clarrie Hayden Show who came to Ederney Townhall. A local talent contest was generally part of their stay and Philomena Begley, of Pomeroy, Co., Tyrone, later known as "Ireland's Queen of Country Music," remembers fondly that as a child she won ten shillings singing a duet with another girl in Clarrie Hayden's Travelling Show. During the 1950s Mullan, Co., Monaghan was able to support a popular Dance Hall which also hosted the popular 'Clarrie Hayden Show', a touring light entertainment show which helped the popular entertainer Val Doonican on his way to fame. These touring parties brought colour to the town. They lived in their touring caravans and sometimes had amusements which they set up as an additional source of revenue. These featured swing boats, pellet gun shooting ranges, flashing lights and loud amplified music of the hits of the day. Invariably they featured very pretty girls heavily made up and many young men deserted their current girlfriends in a vain attempt to woo these glamorous creatures only to have to crawl back to patch up their relationships as the caravans left town. Their shows were slick through practice and often featured plays arranged around ballads such as "The Wild Colonial Boy" and "The Colleen Bawn." They came, they were seen and they conquered and moved on until winter forced them indoors to await another touring season.

It would not be entirely correct to describe these theatricals as "coarse acting" as many who got their first experience of the acting bug went on to star in big city theatres at home and abroad. Based on his experiences in England, Michael Green wrote "The Art of Coarse Acting" when he was involved with amateur dramatics there. Green describes a coarse actor as "one who can remember his lines, but not the order in which they come. One who performs ... amid lethal props." and goes on: "The Coarse Actor's aim is to upstage the rest of the cast. His hope is to be dead by Act Two so that he can spend the rest of his time in the bar. His problems? Everyone else connected with the production." Green began his career as a junior journalist and later he was a sports writer on the Observer and a contributor to the Sunday Times among others. Green is famed for his zany and slightly eccentric behaviour. He is remembered for starting the presses at the *Leicester Mercury* late one Saturday night so that he could run off his own personal copy of the Mercury's sports edition. Green was left somewhat bemused when he was unable to stop the machinery, causing general mayhem all around.

However, if a bit over the top in his judgments, those who appeared on stage enjoyed themselves and survived often share a fund of stories of missing props, missed entrances, incorrect or forgotten lines and a host of other theatrical mishaps. Now in the days of television the likes of Denis Norden presides over comedy shows like *It'll be Alright on the Night* which feature outtakes from British and American sitcoms and foreign advertisements showing what went wrong, famous actors and actresses forgetting their lines or having to shoot multiple scenes through mispronunciation or inappropriate laughter. On our low-tech stages there were no second chances and while there might be a little sympathy for someone's faux pas the rest of the cast would soon show their displeasure if there were too many mistakes regardless of cause.

The faulty prop is a familiar nightmare and "The Down Express" was built around frequent telephone calls to a the railway station set. Tom Costello and Conor Carney of the Pettigo Drama group were there on stage as the curtain rose in the Rock Hall, Ballyshannon. Conor sat at the table reading the paper while Tom went to take the first phone call. Lifting the receiver the whole lot crashed to the floor. The audience warmed to us immediately as they knew we were in deep doda. Tom started into a completely new and unscripted show – "Jeees, would you look at that – what sort of bloody workmen have we these days – they only left an hour ago and the whole damn thing is down – I suppose there isn't a hammer in the place – if you want anything done about here you have to do it yourself – its all right for you reading the paper I have to do everything about here – I'm a bloody slave……..'

All of these rhetorical remarks were addressed to his superior reading the paper who would not have been able to make a coherent response as the paper was high in the air hiding his face and quivering as if in a stiff breeze. Everything got mended eventually and The Down Express steamed on it merry way.

Muscovy Duck - Superstar

In Killeter Hall the Pettigo Players were enacting "The Damsel From Dublin." It was an unlikely tale of a small time crook from Dublin escaping from custody disguised as a woman and ending up in a rural area and staying with Michael John and his elderly widower father. A woman would be useful about the house and since nobody else could be persuaded to play the "female lead" as producer I had to lead from the front in a borrowed two-piece suit and blond wig. It was a long narrow hall and only the front rows were visible as the rest of the presumed audience were shrouded in thick cigarette smoke. I was at an ironing board doing a burlesque version of ironing Michael John's shirt, liberally splashing water in all directions to the especial amusement of the ladies in the audience. Noticing three

L to R. Front row - Isobel Curran, Mamie Faughnan, Mary Colton and Teresa Riordan. Back L to R. Mary Mc Caffrey, Gerry Riordan, Tom Costello, John Cunningham, Josie Shallow, Mick Kilgallon, Eddie Green, Patrick Shallow, Patricia Britton, Brendan Faughnan & Dympna Carr.

small boys engaged in punching each other in the front row I decided to get them to pay attention (the old school teacher coming out in me). I gave them a liberal handful of water which certainly brought them to heel but also shook the audience as it caused a bulb or two in the footlights to go off with a bang and steam to ascend gently to join the smoky mist.

Sometimes you can hear people talking in the audience. In another performance of the same play I could hear this elderly man and his daughter arguing in the front row as to whether or not I was a man in a woman's costume. He was firmly of the opinion that I was a woman (God bless his eyesight) despite her more expert opinion on the matter. Only when I was briefly alone on the stage and reached into an inner pocket and produced a pipe and matches did I hear him say, "Be God, you're right, he is a man." Not much of a compliment for me in either form of transvestism.

In a Ballyshannon production of the musical "Annie Get Your Gun" the drinks were on the house as we all stampeded to the bar to get our shot of whiskey in the form of cold brown tea. We were under orders to "down it in one" so mud in your eye and similar salutations as we threw it back. Except for the last night when some of the non-drinkers had lightly coloured brownish raw poteen in their glasses. Eyes streamed, faces blazed, throats were clutched and a few Confirmation pledges shattered and nobody admitted to the dastardly crime.

In the same show in a one pound raffle among the cast the eight can-can girls had a photograph taken and the winner was to be the person who could identify the girls without seeing the girls' faces – the only clue being their legs. A callow youth of fifteen who helped shift the scenery was the surprise winner – obviously beginner's luck. (There is no point in telling who was asked to take the photograph and thereby removed from the voting list – crudely disenfranchised).

A common saying in the theatre is never if at all possible appear with children or animals. Their unscripted actions invariably cause some form of chaos and our "Down Express" had a Muscovy duck. For some malign reason the playwright required a duck – Michael John's pet duck to wander on to the stage at the end of act one so he could pick it up and pet it. My wife's sister possessed such a pet duck which was used to wandering into the farmhouse following a trail of bread. Accordingly the duck came everywhere with us and was gently tipped out of its box with a little velocity toward Michael John on the stage. Released from the darkness of the box the duck strolled into mid stage, looked around, waggled its tail and promptly shit on the stage – every single time – so we had duck scoot to clean up hurridly to the acclaim of the audience who if they had known the phrase might have shouted "Author, Author" and called for a retake of the scene. So *belatedly, let's hear it for the duck.*

For Brian and Joanne
6-3-2011

L to R - Mick Kilgallon, Tom Costello and John Cunningham.

Never Finish
by Ruthanne Baxter

I'm told by those around me
I never finish anything
Can I help it if my life is incomplete?
I don't see it as a negative
Some do finish things – badly,
I'd like to take 'the end' and hit 'delete'!
Take, for example, my ex-boyfriend
How he ended our relationship was dire
He sent a text, would you believe,
Stating "Soz, was gr8 but it can't go on
Now a barmaid from Ibiza's my desire"
Finishing things can be tricky
They say you can choke on the tail
Though not finishing things academically
Often makes what would have been a pass, a fail.
This sort of thing upsets the parents
"What were you thinking?", "Don't you care?"
Blah, blah, blah
If I finished, I'd have reached my potential
Then have nothing to strive for
Ha, ha, ha!
That said, some things are best when over,
Recessions, root fillings
And wars come to mind
Inoculations, bowl haircuts and Jedward
These things too are best left behind
Partial, incomplete, unfinished
The battle is yet to be won
I was told to write a 40 line poem
But I may choke on the tail so. . .
                        I'm done!

Ode to the Scots 17-03-09
by Ruthanne Baxter

It is not mere luck to be Irish
We are God's chosen few,
That says a lot about me
And a little bit more about you

We've been blessed with the gift of the gab
And have a wit and a spirit of fame,
You've got a defeated rugby team
And the world's leading heart attack shame

We brought the world U2
The greatest band under the sun,
You gave us Fred Goodwin and bagpipes,
Gordon Brown and thistles – nice one!

It must be hard, not being Irish
The No.1, top Celtic race
But as the Welsh too can play rugby
You be proud to be in third place!

NOTE: I was in my third year of working and residing on the East coast of Scotland and had annually displayed a little national pride and faith in the Irish rugby team. This pride was always met with a little amusement by my Scottish colleagues and friends so I was inspired to write this poetic response, to celebrate Ireland winning the Six Nations on St Patrick's Day, 2009.

Poolside Red Alert
by Ruthanne Baxter

The overcast August sky was starting to clear as Dad squeezed the last suitcase into the boot of the car. Mother, who had now actually fastened her seat belt having re-entered the car for the third time, explained that we were going to 'share' our holiday in County Kerry. What this really meant was they would put up with amusement arcades and crazy golf while we would endure sight-seeing and antique shops.

When I say 'we', I refer to myself, the middle child aged 9, with my brother just one year older and my sister a little under 18 months younger – my mum believed in having them one after the other to clear the 'nappy years' in one set phase.

On the second night in 'The Hermitage', our wonderfully rural self-catering cottage, we put it to our parents that the first two days of our 'shared' holiday had been spent doing their things. My father objected to this claim pointing out that the long journey down didn't count and attending church was a family event so, in truth, we were simply owed a day.

Over a bowl of crackling Rice Krispies at suppertime, we started negotiations regarding the agenda for Day 3. A visit to Waterworld in Tralee was agreed, on condition no detours would be taken, thus keeping time spent in the car to a minimum.

Monday was my day to sit in the front seat and navigate. Having studied the *AA Road Map of Ireland* over breakfast I had jotted down the shortest route to Tralee.
It was slightly after eleven thirty when we trooped out of the changing room in Waterworld. With my self-protective nature I went straight to the safety and quiet of the children's pool while Dad accompanied his less fearful, more carefree offspring to the Mega Force Water Tube.

Initially the plan was that Dad would supervise from the top of the tube until my siblings had used up their quota of 10 tube vouchers. However, like giving the last Rolo to someone you love, my little sister insisted Dad had to enjoy this thrilling experience. Using her innocent smile and big, blue eyes persuasively, she gently placed ticket number ten into my father's rough, work-worn farmer's hand.

We gathered excitedly around the shallow pool that represented the arrivals department for tube users. Waiting patiently for Dad we watched as little people, in variously coloured swimsuits, popped out of the tube like Smarties.

Suddenly the cry went up "Someone's stuck!" and our attention was drawn to a large shadow visible on the side of the big, yellow tube.

Just then the shadow began to move rapidly and within seconds our Dad hit the pool like a crocodile devouring its prey, limbs everywhere, splutters sounding from the three foot deep basin of water before us. The drama heightened when the well-toned, attractive, male lifeguard recognised this adult was drowning, not waving, and so stepped into the water up to his mid-calf and offered my panicking father his hand of rescue.

When the crisis had passed, the lifeguard reassured on-lookers all was well, then, reuniting us with our rather shaken Dad this handsome hero, feeling our embarrassment, turned to us with a smile and said, "Parents eh! You can't take them anywhere."

Water Tube Slide

Waterworld Tralee

A LINK TO HER PAST
by Dianne Trimble

Brenda Donnelly copied the words that ran into each other onto the blank space at the top of her computer screen just as her son, John, had written them. When she clicked the piece of plastic that John called a mouse a familiar image appeared. She smiled as she studied the solid, grey building, knowing each arch and window. St Michael's Church looked just as she remembered it before she left Ireland nearly forty years ago.

She'd never spent much time on her computer before her accident. But, since she twisted her ankle a couple weeks ago and had been housebound, she had been exploring its capabilities - surfing the net they called it. That's how she had discovered that her local church had a camera filming the Mass and she could watch it. She was glad to find this link to her normal life.

She didn't know what had prompted her to ask John whether she could see St Michael's on her computer. When she used to visit her sister in Ballylea, she had attended the church. But she hadn't been there since her sister moved to town.

It must be several years since I was last there, she thought, surprised.

Why had she even thought of St Michael's? Maybe John's questions yesterday about her First Communion had started it. His daughter would make her First Communion this Easter. She told him how she remembered kneeling at the altar rail at St Michael's in her shiny satin dress with her best friend, Kate McCusker. The dress was handed down from an older cousin but it was nearly new and she loved it. She had smiled at the memory and John had said it was good to see her smile. Then he had searched for the church's details and had written down the Mass times for her.

She clicked on 'Watch Live' and waited as a

Church of the Sacred Heart, Templemore

white pattern swirled around in the middle of the black screen. Suddenly an image appeared. She heard the sound of heels clicking slowly on tiles. Two elderly women shuffled stiffly up the aisle. Brenda watched the congregation filter into the church in ones and twos.

I've found it in time for Mass, she thought. She leaned back in her chair, pulling her laptop computer closer to her.

As people continued to file into the church Brenda's thoughts strayed to when she was a girl attending Mass with her family. It was more than 40 years ago but she remembered it clearly. As the eldest, it fell to Brenda to help mind the younger children. While listening to the priest, she kept her eye on her siblings, glaring at them if they dared fidget or whisper. Sometimes she would steal a glance across the aisle, trying to catch Martin Corrigan looking at her. If their eyes met his face would crease into a smile before he looked away. She tried to shake off the memory. That was, indeed, a long time ago.

Brenda focussed on the computer screen again. Most of the congregation were now seated. A slim, grey haired man walked up the aisle. There was something familiar about him. She leaned forward, peering more closely at the screen. As he slid into a pew a couple rows from the altar she caught a glimpse of his face. This man was obviously older but he was very like Martin. She was nearly sure it was him.

Her forehead creased in a frown. She knew he moved to Belfast soon after she left for Manchester. So what was he doing back in Ballylea? He must be visiting, she thought.

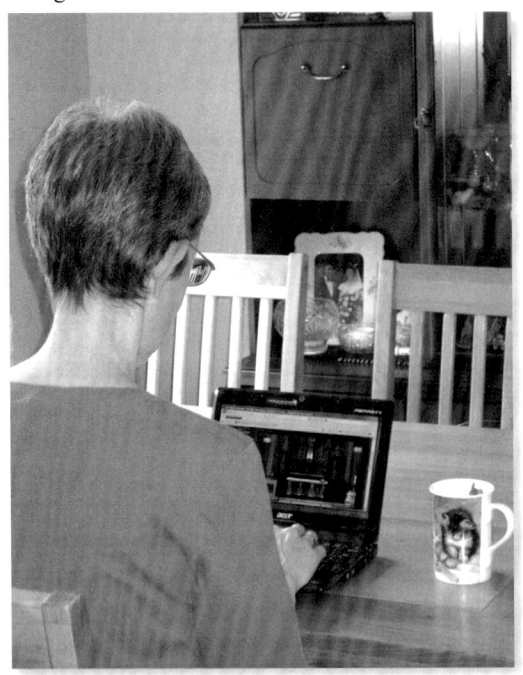

Brenda shifted in her chair, trying to concentrate. The priest welcomed the congregation. As she listened to the familiar words of the Mass, her thoughts drifted back again to her girlhood in Ballylea.

She'd known Martin as long as she could remember. His family ran the village pub and shop. Her mother often sent her to the shop for messages. The summer she was sixteen he often flirted with her when she called to the shop and at the August Carnival he had asked her to dance. During the next two years they spent more and more time together. Everyone thought they would marry one day.

And we would have if I hadn't

been so foolish, she thought ruefully.

The recessional hymn brought her back to the present and she focussed on her computer screen again. The priest and altar servers processed towards her and out of the church. The brief silence that followed was quickly replaced by rustlings and bumps as people gathered their belongings and left. The grey haired man stood up. As he turned to walk up the aisle she held her breath then let it out sharply. It was Martin.

When had she last seen him? It must have been the night before she took the ferry to England. He'd asked her not to go but she had told him stiffly that everything had been arranged with her aunt. Even when he explained about Biddy O'Neill, her pride would not allow her to change her mind.

She couldn't listen to the gossip. Martin had been spending far too much time at the O'Neill's house. Everyone knew that he was walking out with her, not Biddy. Martin had explained that Biddy's mother needed help with the heavy work around the farm. The widow couldn't afford to pay a farm hand so he'd offered to pitch in when he wasn't wanted at the pub. Though his parents weren't farmers, he'd always loved helping on his uncle's farm. So he didn't mind calling to the O'Neills several times each week. But his visits had not gone unnoticed; Brenda had heard the whispered conversations in the village. She was humiliated and decided she couldn't stay and listen to their talk.

During the next few weeks it became a habit for Brenda to switch on her computer in time for St Michael's Sunday Mass. After so many years away, she enjoyed tuning into Mass in her hometown church. And when her ankle had improved enough for her to get out, she went to Vigil Mass Saturday evening at her local church and spent Sunday morning in front of her computer screen. She justified this by telling herself that Mass at a traditional church like St Michael's made her feel at home. She loved seeing the intricately carved altar and graceful statues poised near it. The architecture awed her, making her feel humble and grateful in God's presence. Her local church's modern style didn't make her feel quite the same.

Telling herself this, she tried not to notice how eagerly she scanned the worshippers filing out of the church, looking for Martin. Each week she had spotted his slim form walking down the aisle. She noticed that he chatted with other parishioners but he was always alone. She wondered what he was doing in Ballylea.

*****

As the weeks passed Brenda's thoughts turned increasingly to her hometown. She wondered how her good friend, Kate, was getting on these days. As she switched off her computer after Mass one Sunday she decided she would phone Kate. They used to write at least once a month but had fallen out of the habit these past few years. Now they phoned each other a few times each year, on special occasions such as Christmas and Easter.

After lunch Brenda lifted the phone. She knew Kate would be sitting by the fire relaxing as her adult children tidied up after the Sunday meal. Kate sounded surprised and pleased to hear her voice. They chatted about their lives and the news of the village. Brenda almost felt as if she'd never been away.

"Since I hurt my ankle I've been tuning into Mass at St Michael's. It's grand to see our church after all these years," Brenda said.

"Well, isn't that amazing – you're over in England and with us at St Michael's at the same time," Kate replied.

After a moment's hesitation, Brenda said, "I noticed Martin Corrigan in the congregation. Has he come back to Ballylea?"

"It must be ages since I last talked to you, Brenda!" Kate exclaimed. "Indeed he has. He took early retirement from his job in Belfast and came back to Ballylea. Boyle's farm was for sale last spring and he bought it. Do you mind that he always had a notion of farming? It was no bother to him to help Biddy's mother when he was a lad."

Brenda forced herself to keep her tone neutral. "I remember that, surely," she replied.

Kate paused for a moment before she added, "I mind you weren't keen on him spending so much time at the O'Neills when you were walking out with him."

"Folk were talking. You know how it was. I hated all their talk about Martin and Biddy."

"Well, you know it was only ever talk. Martin never had eyes for anyone but you. He was heartsore when you left Ballylea."

"I know. Before I went to Aunt Mary he asked me to stay but I just couldn't listen to the gossip anymore. Looking back it seems a silly reason to finish with him and leave."

"Hindsight's always clearer," Kate agreed.

"How's his wife and children adjusting to farm life?" Brenda asked, changing the subject.

"Dear me, how could I have forgotten to mention it? His wife, Valerie, died a couple years ago. Not long after your Barry. His children are all grown and away from home."

"Oh, I'm sorry to hear that. I never even heard she was ill."

"No, she wasn't. It was quite unexpected. His children – there's three of them – visit him often. One of his sons has a knack for farming, like his father."

"That's grand," Brenda said, still assimilating the news about his wife's death.

"So, when are you coming for that long overdue visit you've promised me?" Kate asked. "Your ankle must be well mended by now."

"It is much better and, with the weather getting milder maybe I could come over early next month?"

"Grand. You make the arrangements and let me know when to pick you up at Belfast Airport."

*****

A few minutes before Mass started Brenda followed Kate and her husband, Sean, up the centre aisle. Since she arrived in Ballylea a few days ago she had anticipated Sunday morning with a mixture of excitement and dread. She tried not to think about Martin. She didn't know what she would say to him.

As she slid into the pew after Kate she spotted Martin's grey head bent in prayer two rows ahead of her. During Mass she tried not to stare at him and, when asked to offer the Sign of Peace, feeling flustered and sure her face must be beet red, she quickly turned to the pew behind her and shook the nearest lady's hand.

When Mass ended Brenda led her friends to the door. She smiled to herself when the priest, who was new to the parish, shook her hand and welcomed her as a visitor. Walking down the steps she turned to speak to Kate and found herself looking into Martin's warm, hazel eyes.

"It's good to see you, Brenda."

"And you too, Martin. I don't be in Ballylea often now the family's all away."

"I know. I can't even mind how long it's been since I last saw you."

Brenda took a deep breath and made a decision. "It's not been that long since I last saw you, Martin," she replied. Martin looked at her quizzically.

Brenda explained how she had tuned into Masses at St Michael's and had spotted him in the congregation. She concluded saying, "Seeing you here again reminded me of all that happened in the past. I was very foolish in my youth. Pride made me act rashly. I wanted a chance to tell you that."

"Well, then, why don't we get a cup of tea? We've lots to catch up on."

Brenda and Martin smiled at each other with an understanding that bridged the last forty years.

Cahir McKeown's Early Memories
as told to Dianne Trimble with excerpts from his book, *Enniskillen Reminiscences*
(book excerpts in italics)

I would have been born in the middle of the town above where Staks* is, in 1924. We were a family of seven. There was four brothers and myself and two sisters and my father and mother - there'd be nine altogether. We moved to Darling Street when I was very young. It was a peaceful place to be living.

I went to St Michael's [primary school] but to the Convent first. When you were very small you were at Babies and High Infants [as] they called the three classes before you went down to the Brothers' school. The Brothers' school was primary one, two, three, four, five and six and they had an intermediate school** where St Michael's Community Hall is, behind the Clinton Centre. Then, when you were finished at fourteen, you went to secondary school.

It was Presentation Brothers, they could be called Christian Brothers too, but it was the Presentation order of brothers that taught.

There was a great brother up in fifth and sixth class. He was the name of Brother Claver and he didn't use the cane or any [such] persuasion. But he gave me a great interest in singing even to the present time. The University of the Third Age has a great choir of people, maybe twenty including myself, and we do a lot of singing.

The late Rev Bro Claver was the choir-master in the old school at the East Bridge which acquired sadder fame in later years. At 2.30 pm every day, the school books were packed away and we went into the small room at the back of our classroom every day for choir practice.

First, we would go through the scales, do, re, me, fa, so, la, tee, do and once our choir-master tapped the tuning fork on his thumb there would be complete silence. Our lead singer, the late Jack Keenan - he went on to become Principal of St Joseph's Secondary School- took the key for the particular song we were going to sing. It was an honour to be in the choir. Boys unable to sing had to stand at the side and read books. We were always kept on our toes with the interest generated in the yearly competitions at the local Feis. Invariably the final would be between the Convent of Mercy School and St Michael's and generally St Michael's would win the coveted prize.

To give people an idea of the preparation - we would have to come in on Saturdays for practice lasting three hours. Bro Claver would have records and play them on the wind-up old "His Masters Voice" gramophone. One set piece was "The Last Rose of Summer" by Count John McCormack, and we would then be expected to give a rendering.

Brother Claver got Miss Brown from the Model School, before we went into the feis, for to give him ideas and listen to his choir. It was an ecumenical type of town then. *Nothing was left to chance before we would sing in public. The late Harry Hudson's (photographer) job was to pass around sweets bought by Bro Claver. These were sugar acid drops in a large silver can and they helped to clear our throats and make our voices sweeter. Some of the functions we attended and sang at included the Fermanagh Feis in the County Hall***, Enniskillen - now the gymnasium of the Fermanagh College of Further Education, a charity concert in the Regal Cinema at which Hubert Valentine, a leading concert tenor of the '30s in Ireland, sang.*

At this particular concert, the Brother was asked why he kept me in the front row. He said "He's a fair singer, but he gives a good impression because he opens his mouth wide." There were also concerts in Tempo and Derrygonnelly, along with religious processions at the convent and in Newtownbutler. At these concerts was another great singer, the late Mr Kennedy, the father of Joe Kennedy, of Derrin Road, Enniskillen, who trained in Dublin. Other singers in the choir, apart from myself, that come to mind were Jackie Wardsman (Canada), Michael Love, Austin Drumm, Jimmy Stennett, Jimmy Cleary, Paddy Fitzsimmons, John Dooris, Billie Drumm, Paddy McCusker, Harry Ralph and Thomas McCallion - to name but a few off-hand. Bro Claver was before his time in the educational system. He used to let us walk around the room and ask questions of other boys. If you were weak in English, he would place you with a boy who was good at English - but the two subjects he required complete silence for were drawing and singing.

Frank Harvey used to sit along with me in the same seat in the school in fifth and sixth class. Since I was always working, I didn't do much reading and that was bad for English. Frank Harvey was a great reader, but he wasn't too good at sums. So he [Brother Claver] put him along with me so that you could copy off each other. There was no such thing as copying in his idea of things. One was learning the other. And Frank Harvey finished up working in the bank in Donegal.

When I was younger we used to play around the Broad Meadow. The Broad Meadow is still there but it used to be all rushes at that time. There was a soccer field, (Corinthians football team practiced there) and then the Police ground was in the Broadmeadow too. They had their training ground - they had a pavilion and all in it. In about 1936 the police came to Enniskillen to the police barracks. It was an army barracks previous to that. Enniskillen, being a garrison town, there was always army in it but the last army left in 1928.

I would have took part in the football but you wouldn't have had much time. And even it was a poor enough time - you know the way the young people have an outfit now, you would hardly get a pair of football boots. And there was a lot of us in our family. It was enough to keep us - we were well fed and looked after but that [sports] come secondary. That's why we just played with our own boots. And then it [the Broadmeadow] was a dumping ground as well. People had small stuff and it would be carted down. From the 1920s to the 1940s at the back of the Legion and where the Forum is now it was all dumped with old stuff.

As I've said, I lived close the chapel in Darling Street. I was an altar-boy and Mass would be at 8 o'clock in the morning. There'd be a number of boys and you might be put on for a month. You might do 2 months in the year for the whole month, every day.

Living near St Michael's Church was an advantage. My good mother would have me out on time for 8 o'clock Mass with a clean white surplus and black soutane. I enjoyed serving the good priests of the parish, even not realising that I was serving God, my Creator. The tradition of serving Mass as an altar boy was much enjoyed in years gone by. First you had to learn the Latin responses, which were difficult enough but, with practice improved as you went along.

There were four priests in Enniskillen and there's still only four. There was Fr Meegan, Fr Duignan, Fr O'Daly and Monsignor Tierney, the parish priest who was from Donagh. The other priests were mainly from Monaghan at that time. *Some of the boys who served with me were Frank Harvey, Gerald Goane, Frank and Joe McPhail and Jack Keenan.*

Fr Tierney would bring us on a yearly outing on his large motorboat, driven by the Sexton, James Muncy, to Devenish. This was by way of his thanks to us for serving

St Michael's Church interior. Credit Gail McGowan Photographer

during the year. Fr Meegan, from Inniskeen, Co Monaghan, my mother's country, was Spiritual Director of the Arch Confraternity, who also served on Lough Derg in the Pilgrimage Season, could give you a speedy run at Mass and devotions. By contrast, Fr C O'Daly was slow. Holy Hour would be Holy Hour and a half! A fluent Irish speaker, he was instrumental in planting the many trees around the Old Gaelic Field on the Sligo Road. Fr Duignan, from Ballybay, a cousin of Dr Smith, loved conversation with all people as he walked about the town and knew everybody by name. In those days the clergy walked or cycled to do their calls - except on Sunday, when Joe Flanagan supplied the taxi to Cradien and Lisbellaw. They were also chaplains to the workhouse, which had an Oratory at the end of the large dining hall, with Michael Love serving, as he lived not far away, in Mill Street also the brothers Thomas, Eddie and Paddy Quinn who lived in the houses closeby.

Easter and Christmas ceremonies were happy occasions. For these you needed at least twenty altar boys. It was lovely to wear the red soutane supplied for these set occasions. Rich vestments for a great ritual. The three curates assisted Monsignor Tierney, Master of Ceremonies, with Fr Duignan as chantor. James Muncy was kept busy, arranging everything and keeping us in order. I had occasion to serve in the Convent of Mercy at a Children of Mary ceremony. The Monsignour said to me: "Watch you do not knock some of the flower pots over or slip on the highly polished floor". He knew I was an awkward boy anyway but I got away without a mishap!

NOTES:
* - At that time the Co-op shop was located on the site where Staks is now.
** - St. Michael's Intermediate School opened in 1903 in the building that is now St. Michael's Community Centre (behind the Clinton Centre).
*** - The site where South West College, formerly Fermanagh College of Further Education, is located has had several uses over the years. When the nineteenth century Gaol closed the council offices were built on the site; the County Hall was located in this building.

Judgement Scene, St Michael's entrance. Credit Gail McGowan Photographer

Watching for a Drink
by Sean McElgunn

In 1965 I was back in Ireland for a break and stationed in Clonard in Belfast. In October I received notice to assist in a parish mission in Templemore, in north Tipperary. The 'old man' Matt, was from Dubin's Northside. He had spent most of his life in India; like me he was going back out East. Matt spoke quite 'posh' English but, when he got going in full flow on a yarn, he effortlessly lapsed into Dublinese that would put Berty Ahern to shame. We were staying with the PP. One of my jobs was to lecture the budding Guards; that was the year that the college was moved there from the Depot in the Phoenix Park. I didn't notice anyone nodding off but I doubt if they took my words of wisdom too seriously.

Every night we listened to the 10 o'clock news and the housekeeper made tea. Matt loved a night-cap but the PP was a teetotaller, anathema on the drink. Every night I could see Matt eyeing the Paddys twinkling in the firelight in the corner cupboard. Not a gig out of the old dry stick, though he'd have to be stone blind not to notice the body language. Matt made discreet enquiries; the housekeeper said the whiskey was there on sufferance for the very odd time the Bishop chanced to call.

Wednesday night of the second week Matt could stand it no longer. He had said to me earlier, 'Watch me moving the stiff-necked oul so-and-so.' When the news was over he launched into a rambling yarn about Lord Erne, concocted from whole cloth, I suspect, for the occasion. It seems Lord Erne had these vast estates in Fermanagh and Tyrone. He lived, of course, in London but once a year he made it his business to visit the tenants. An ancient retainer would be waiting to take him around, who made sure his worship was 'treated' properly on the way. Naturally, his lordship would be feeling merry by the end of the day; he grew very fond of the old man, who had a standing invitation to visit the great Town House in London. Likely story!

But marvels never cease. It came to pass that a granddaughter was getting married, and in London! With plenty of time on his hands Oul Darby set out to find the Town House, and by some minor miracle found it. The same gentleman (the butler) kept ignoring him in his shabby clothes, as he let visitors in and out. Finally, Darby sneaked in when he got the snooty fellow's back turned, and hid away in a corner. He sat there for ages.

By sheer chance Lord Erne spotted him, as he returned from personally ushering out some particular friend. He rushed over, extremely embarrassed and smothered him with welcomes. 'And how is everybody back home in Fermanagh? the family? and the neighbours? and the stock? All were fine. There was just one wee problem. What was the problem? asked His Highness, anxiously. It was the sow. Was she sick? No, she was in tip-top form. She had 15 healthy bonhams. Well, what could be the problem then? She had only 14 tits. Aw, mercy save the poor last starving creature; what is he doing? To tell you the God's truth, your Worship, he is doing exactly the same as me, he's sitting on his arse waiting for a drink.

With a snort the old fogey shot up out of the chair and headed for Paddy in the press. And Matt winked at me. He's long gone, God rest him, but if he's listening, he'll know that every word I have said is true. Any lies are his.

The Sun Shone
by Julie Richmond

The sun shone brightly
The stream gently flowed
Over the smooth rocks beneath,

The park, desolate,
No one in sight,

The fledglings screaming for food,
Parents in hunt for big juicy succulent worms,

The stray dog,
Enjoys time running
And jumping,
Playing with empty cans,
From park bins

With Thanks
by Julie Richmond

Your generosity warms my heart,
I wasn't expecting but now I'm receiving.

My actions were given out of the kindness of my heart,
I didn't want you being pushed and pulled at every part,
So I thought I would do my part.

More knowledge I received
A teaching well comprehended,
While new relationships began to bloom.

Thanks be to all our great teachers
Who give up their time and vitality,
To pass on their gifts, talents and knowledge
This enables us to reach new paths,

And in return we see their satisfaction,
A continued desire for more wisdom
And knowledge to feed our beings
Keeps us strong

Moorehead's Gander
by Winston Graydon

Sandy Gray and Paddy Finn, old neighbours, were passing the time sitting on the old stone bridge and chatting about this and that.

'Boys Sandy, did ye ever see as wicked a gander as that one a Mooreheads?'

'I've seen some wicked ganders in me time, Paddy, but that's the worst I've ever seen. As wicked as a wasp!'

'Well Sandy, I was comin' down the road the other day on the bicycle and I could see no sign a the gander at first and a thought to me self, 'I'm alright the day, the gander mustn't be about'. The next thing a knew it came out at such a tare… you wouldn't believe the speed of it… half flyin' and half runnin'… its feet hardly touchin' the ground. Then, didn't it make one great blinge at me leg and am tellin' you, Sandy, I was glad to get away from it! I got a right bite through me trousers an' all!'

'Aye an' you were lucky you were on a bicycle, Paddy, for anyone walkin', well, they have no way a gettin' out of its road. One day I was walkin' down the road Paddy, never thinkin' of the gander and ye know thon gap in the hedge into the field? Well, the first thing I seen of the gander was in under the hedge an' it was just sittin' rale quiet, not movin' a muscle, just settin' me…. ye know the way an oul cat would be settin' a bird? Sittin' quiet but at the same time ready to pounce. An' boys Paddy, it flew at me like a clockin' hen! An' me swingin' the shoppin' bag a was carryin' all 'roun' me an' tryin' to get a kick at it at the same time…. but the bird is fearless Paddy… an it kept goin' at me for long enough. A thought a would never get away past it, an' it followin' me down the road. A was nearly afraid to look back, Paddy, when a did get clear, in case it would have another go at me!'

'Wouldn't ye wonder what makes it so cross, Sandy?'

'It must be that it sees that place as its own patch, an' just guards it with its life.'

'Ye know Sandy, there's people that'll not come past it at all. They go away 'roun' by Aghavea church or the broad road by Brookeborough to avoid the gander.

'Ah sure Paddy, there's childer comin' home from Littlemount school that have jumped the hedge to get out of its road…. an' ran away over the fields to get home. Someone was tellin' me a funny story about a man that was comin' home from Brookeborough one evenin' with a lot a drink in him. It appears he had been drinkin' most of the day in one a the pubs in the village - maybe in all three a them. Anyway there was an open air meetin' in the village that particular evenin' and this man, Willie was his name, had just come out a the pub and was staggerin' along the footpath. Well, the preacher was layin' it on hot an' heavy about the demon drink, 'an' the smokin', an' where those who were at it would be goin' and I suppose when he saw Willie staggerin' along, an' him carryin' a kishogue a drink under his arm, he gave it all the more stick! Anyway, Willie made his way on out the Aghavea road and I suppose all this would a been runnin' through his head, especially as he passed the Soldier's Point, and it was just a few hundred yards further on to where Moorehead's gander always made his attack. The light was startin' to fade now,

Paddy, and I suppose Willie wasn't seein' the best anyway with all the drink he had on him. As he told someone later, the next thing he knew was this great flappin' a wings behind him, somethin' tuggin' at the leg of his trousers and in the fadin' light he could just about make out a great big pair of white wings.

'By God!' gasped Willie to himself, 'The preacher was right but a thought ye might a waited til a died, Oul Nick, before ye would a come for me!' and on he staggered up to the cross roads. 'I was glad,' he said later, 'when Oul Nick let go a me – an' a thought to meself, there must be some purpose for me here on earth yet! But he never let go a the kishogue a stout. He wasn't goin' to drop that for Oul Nick or anyone …. a think that was what Willie was proud about after the whole ordeal.'

'That's a scary one, Sandy. The oul gander is bad enough in broad daylight when you're sober, let alone with a load a drink on ye, comin' on to night and the fear a the Devil on ye.'

'There was another man who once turned on the gander himself,' said Paddy. 'He was a brave man, Sandy.'

'He was, Paddy, but he had a big cudgel of a stick in his hand and was flayin' all roun' him with it and a believe the gander was side steppin' him like a boxer and every chance it got it went for his leg and he was shoutin' about this bein' a dangerous thing to be doin' comin' up to Christmas. 'If I get the hold a ye, you'll get your oul neck pulled an' be in the pot for Christmas day!' but I believe he had to give up and go on out of its road and the gander chased after him as defiant as ever.'

'Well Sandy, I think I'll keep out a that gander's way in the future for Moorehead was tellin' me it's far better than any dog about the place and it doesn't need to do any barkin', for when anyone sees it they know to give it a wide berth. The postman stands well out a the road til someone comes to him ….. I think he's had a few runs in with the gander in his time. I believe it's startin' to run at cars now so that could be the end of it.'

'It could indeed, Paddy, but I suppose the moral a the story is, 'watch out for the devil - he comes in all sorts a disguises - even in the form a Moorehead's gander!'

<blockquote>
Fearing neither man or beast,
kick or stick made no retreat
Anyone who passed that way,
very soon became his prey
Men and women, drunk or sober
were no match for Moorehead's gander
</blockquote>

Cisteog – term often used for a parcel or 'stash' of drink (given in the dictionary as a small chest or casket. The older dictionary gives it a special meaning in Donegal as a small basket in which rush-light candles were kept before use - it describes this as being made of wicker with a board at either end.)

The South-Fermanagh Almanack and Directory 1896
by Dermot Maguire

Along with the Newtownbutler Herald (see *Fermanagh Miscellany 2010*) this was the other publication printed and published by that enterprising 'merchant' of main street Newtownbutler, Robert Maguire. Though directories, gazetteers, almanacks and such like journals first appeared in the 18th century, it was in the 19th century that they became popular. I suppose it was all part of the Victorian urge to collect, categorise and disseminate information useful for life and living. Many were national in scope - Thom's Directory and Old Moore's Almanack are two well known ones. Others were county based, such as Lowe's County Fermanagh. A Guide and Directory, published in 1880. Examples, such as this South-Fermanagh Almanac and Directory, which cover a smaller area than a county, are rare. Its orbit encompassed Maguiresbridge, Brookeborough, Rosslea, Clones and Belturbet, as well as Newtownbutler, Donagh, Magheraveeley and Crom. Like the Newtownbutler Herald, surviving copies appear to be extremely rare.

Townhall Street, Newtownbutler

Like many such publications, it sought to be informative and entertaining, as well as an opportunity for both the proprietor and local businesses to advertise their goods. The almanack part, at the beginning, gives the usual information about festivals, feast days and anniversaries, bank holidays, phases of the moon, eclipses, as well as the Sportsman's Calendar, the Jewish Calendar, the Mahometan Calendar and a section on stamps, taxes and excise duties. The central 'directory' part of it contains, as it claims on the cover, 'Names of Principal Merchants, Farmers, &.c.,' A brief historical and archaeological account is given for each of the towns and villages and the main buildings of note are mentioned. Also typical of such journals are the photographs and illustrations of notable buildings and places such as, Chatsworth, Carnarvon Castle, Alton Towers and York Minster.

While the main focus of this article will be on the 'directory' lists of merchants in each town and farmers in their vicinities, I would like to give you a flavour of the other information it provides on each town and village. We are told Rosslea has seven grocers, but, strangely, no butcher. It also has a good corn and flax mill. In its vicinity 'in its deep glens will be found a numerous peasantry of singular habits, and possessing great originality of character.' Clones, with a population of 2,710, had four hotels, three banks, a Loan Fund Office, a handsome market-house and townhall, gas works, flax and saw-mills, an artificial supply of water from Carn Hollow and a workhouse. The piece on Belturbet was, 'specially written for this Almanack by the Rev. Robert Leech' of Drumlane Rectory. The Rev. Leech speaks of the O'Reillys, Fitzpatricks and Kennedys, and then exthols the virtues of the names Hamilton, Montgomery, Stewart, and a host of others, as well as the locals - Saundersons and Crichtons.

Lisnaskea Lower

Lisnaskea is described as 'well built and prosperous,' with a workhouse, Ulster Bank, Loan Fund Bank, Rent Office and Townhall, as well as the railway station. It goes on to say, 'the late Lord Erne took a deep and practical interest in the town of Lisnaskea.' Brookborough is described as a 'pretty little town.' It tells us, 'Aghalun Castle, the

R & J BRADSHAW,

Grocers, Bakers, Hardware & Seed

MERCHANTS,

LISNASKEA & NEWTOWNBUTLER.

Iron, Timber, Slates; English, Scotch, & Smiths' Coal. Richardson Bros,' Goulding's, and Packord's Manures.

—AGENT FOR—

Star Life Assurance Soc., & Equitable Fire Insurance Co.

ROBT. MAGUIRE

Letterpress Printer, Stationer, &c

NEWTOWN BUTLER.

TENDERS hearty Thanks to the Public for the very liberal, and yearly increasing, support which his Press has received ever since its establishment. In order to keep pace with the rapid growth of the business, he has recently Enlarged his Office, and Increased his Plant by the addition of New Machinery and Type. He is now in a position to satisfactorily execute every class of job, from a Visiting Card to a Poster 30 inches long by 20 wide; and at Prices generally as Low as Belfast or Dublin Houses.

SAMUEL R. MURPHY,

Draper, Grocer, Druggist,

GENERAL HARDWARE AND HOUSE-FURNISHING,

China, Delph, Glass, Seed & Provision Merchant,

BROOKEBOROUGH.

Millinery, Dress and Mantle-making on the Premises

HEARSE & FUNERAL REQUISITES SUPPLIED.

☞ SPECIAL Value in TEAS,

At 1/8, 2/-, 2/4, 2/6, and 2/8 per pound.

Plank & Iron, Coal & Slates. Bone Manure, and Shipping Agent.

HUGH MAGUIRE,

—GENERAL DRAPER,—

Diamond, † CLONES, † Diamond,

Has Always in Stock a Large Selection of

New & Fashionable Goods,

Suitable for the Various Seasons.

Dress-making on the Most Approved & Modern System,

DONE ON THE PREMISES.

H. M. hereby conveys his Thanks to his numerous Customers, for their Patronage in the past, and hopes to merit a continuance of same.

---

remains of which were removed not many years ago, stood in a field close by . . .' We are told that 'the little hamlet' of Donagh has, 'an ancient graveyard, R.C. chapel, school, several small shops, good corn and flax mills, a Post Office and a blacksmiths' forge.' Magheraveely is, 'chiefly remarkable on account of possessing an ancient graveyard in which both Protestants and Roman Catholics bury their dead.' Also, 'it has an excellent National School at Midhill, and an Orange Hall (erected in 1895) at the Knox.' Last, but not least, we have Newtownbutler. We are told, (remember that this is Robert Maguire's home town), it has been 'much admired for its position, its wide and clean streets, its substantial house-property, and the peaceful character of its intelligent and industrious inhabitants.' He also notes the presence of the Willow Park Creamery - one of the earliest in Ulster. Mention is made of Lanesborough Lodge, Castle Saunderson, and the Druid's Temple. He informs us that 'during the summer months great numbers of excursionists pass through Newtownbutler on their way to historic Crom.'

Now for the directory part of the Almanack. Looking down these lists of merchants, tradesmen and farmers, you are struck by the variety of goods sold and trades practiced. It telescopes you back to a time, just a hundred odd years ago, when so much was grown and made locally. As well as farming, there were many occupations related to it in some way: the fowl and butter merchants, the pig and cattle dealers, the victuallersbutchers, the corn mills. But this 'old world' was on the brink of change even then and within a generation or so many specialist crafts people, such as the watchmaker, cooper, saddler, coachbuilder, crochet maker and shoemaker would be no more.

As well as the variety of shops and trades, you notice the high number of publicans, grocers and drapers. In 1896 there were twenty seven publicans in Clones and ten in Lisnaskea, yet just two in each of Newtownbutler and Maguiresbridge. What also catches the eye are the number of grocers who combine with something else: grocer-postmaster, grocer-leather merchant, grocer-draper, grocer-hardware, but more numerous than any of these, the spirit-grocer - the famous old pub-grocery of Irish towns. Then you have the unusual: the rag-merchant, the gas manager, the white smith [tinsmith], the photographer (Miss Galway of Clones), the sheriff's bailiff (Henry Welch, Maguiresbridge), and a Henry Morton of Belturbet who was a 'maker of mineral water.'

Except for the villages of Roslea, Magheraveely and Donagh, all of these towns were served by the railway. Clones and Belturbet were important railway centres; Maguiresbridge was served by both the GNR and the Clogher Valley line. The railway gave steady employment to a good few people, linesmen, signal men, porters, managers, as well as labourers and carters who drew the goods from the station to the shops and beyond.

Maguiresbridge

The Directories

Rosslea

Brannigan, Bernard, grocer
Cadden, Edward, grocer
Cox, John, merchant, post-office
Conlay, Patrick, carpenter
Darcy, - dispensary medical doctor
Deering, John, grocery and spirits
Greadon, Joseph, draper, clerk P.S.
Graham, John, blacksmith
Hazlitt, William, corn mills
Miss Keenan, grocer and publican
Larndnier, the Misses, dressmakers
Lytle, Francis, farmer
Magilly, Michael, shoemaker
Martin, Thomas, shoemaker
Mowen, John, blacksmith
Murray, Patrick, spirit-grocer
McManus, John, grocer and baker
McMahon, Mrs. Dressmaker
McPhilips, Hugh, farmer, roadmaker
Nixon, William, Rosslea flax mills
Sloan, John, grocer
Whitsit, Mrs. landowner

Clones

Clones Directory

The Diamond

Bank of Ireland – H. E. Swayne, agent
Beatty, Mrs., woollen draper
Black, John, spirit merchant
Church of Ireland – Archibald Finlay
Fleming & Co., J, drapers
Gillespie, James, medical doctor
Gibson, Wm., grocer and druggist
Gough, John, hotel proprietor
Graham, Geo. F., auctioneer
Henry, R., medical doctor
Henry, Wm., medical doctor
Kerr, Charles, woollen draper
Lowe, H., grocer & jeweller
Knight, Michael, solicitor
Maguire, E. & F. spirit grocers
Maguire, Hugh, draper
Murray, E. P. J.P., chemist
Murphy, Henry, solicitor
Nicholl, T. & J., merchants
Northern Bank – A. Dudgeon, manager
Parke, Wm. A., solicitor
Pringle, John, butter merchant
Robinson, John, Temperance Hotel
Ulster Bank, J. Galloway, manager
Woods & Co., Wm., drapers

Monaghan Road

Presbyterian Church – Rev. J. Gass
Brogan, John, Victualler

Analore Street

Brogan, Thomas, victualler
Cockings, W. & C., spirit grocers
Ferguson, W. N. & Sons
Gill, Miss, teacher National School
Keirans & Co., Felix, merchants
Kearns, John, carpenter
Maguire, Edward, carpenter
McCullagh, James, mason
McKeaney, John, spirit grocer
Noble, John & Sons, coachbuilders
Reilly, Edward, pig dealer
Williamson, David, gas manager

Abbey Lane

Hammond, Mrs., lodging-house
Jordan, George, car driver
Kavanagh, Wm., lodging-house
Kennedy, Francis, lodging-house
McKenny, J., blacksmith

Whitehall Street

Armstrong, Mrs., Lennard Arms Hotel
Bright, John, merchant tailor
Brownlow, Mrs., property owner
Cassidy, Edward, auctioneer
Coulson, Miss A, workhouse matron
Crawford, John, process server
Dalton, J., spirit dealer
Doris, James, veterinary surgeon
Kelly, Mrs., court-house keeper
Lendrum, James, shoemaker
McAviney, Peter, butter merchant
McCabe, John, publican
McVitty, J. & Son, grocers
Noble, Thomas, grocery & lodgings
Nugent, Miss, lodging-house
Pharr, J. H. spirit grocer
Presho, J. W., crochet lace merchant
Robinson, Joseph, watchmaker
Storey, Richard, shoemaker
Tierney, doctor, J. P.
Turner, Wm., clerk of petty sessions
Wilson, James, printer, &c.
Wiggins, Thomas, workhouse master

Cara Street

Brady, Mary, publican
Carson, David, teacher N. S.
Campbell, John, fashionable tailor
Connolly, Catherine, publican
Courtney, Wm., tinsmith
Doherty, John, publican
Martin, Owen, fowl merchant
Manning, Isaac, lodging-house keeper

Morgan, Joseph, land agent
Murphy, Owen, rag merchant
Stratton, Mrs.

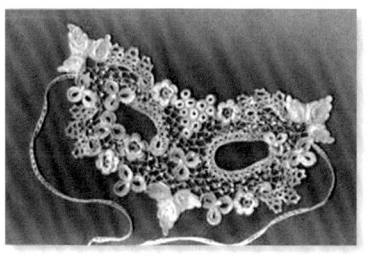

Clones Lace

Fermanagh Street

Armstrong, Wm. Henry, grocer
Bowes, Joseph, grocer
Boyle, Johnston, butter merchant
Brady, John, grocer and publican
Bussell, John, grocer and publican
Clinton, James, boot merchant
Connolly, Wilson, tailor
Coffee, Thomas, publican
Coyle, Mrs., lodging-house keeper
Cross, James, shoemaker
Duggan, Crichton, commercial hotel
Earls, Wm., grocer & leather merchant
Fee, Patrick, fancy warehouse
Ferguson, James & Son, saddlers
Gordon, Hugh, clothier
Hayes, Jas., grocer and postmaster
Hall, Benjamin, general merchant
Hall, Charles, jeweller
Kennedy, Miss I., grocer
Kennedy, George, shoemaker
Kierans, Terence, publican
Kierans, Patrick, general merchants
Little, George, grocer
Little, Miss, publican
Martin & Co., M., drapers
Magovern, T., publican and auctioneer
Maguire, Philip, grocer and publican
Murphy, Owen, saddler
McAviney, Jas., & Co, butter merchts.

McAviney, Thomas, victualler
McCarney, Patrick, publican
McCarney, Peter, publican
McCutcheon, Alexander, baker
McDermott, Miss, confectioner
McDermott, Mrs., grocer & publican
McDermott, J. M. solicitor
McDermott, Miss M., milliner
McDonald, John, Beleek Warehouse
McElroy, Hugh, tailor
McGrain, Thomas, cattle dealer
McPhilips, Richard, victualler
McPhilips, Richard, jun., auctioneer
Nicholl Brothers, grocers
Nicholl, Simon, crochet merchant
Slowey, Patrick, grocer
Toner, Philip, confectioner
Welsh, Samuel, whitesmith
Wiggins, William, woollen draper

Clones Round Tower

Pound Hill

R. C. Church - Rev. Canon O'Neil, P.P.
Rev. M. O'Doherty, C.C.
Rev. L. O'Keirans, C.C.
Keary, Samuel, grocer

Rev. Jas., Gibson, Methodist Minister
Mr. McMahon, teacher N.S.

Newtownbutler Road

John Mitchell, stationmaster, GNR
Barnes, J., coffee tavern
Cullen, Rev. John, Methodist Manse
Galway, Miss, photographer
McMahon, Wm., builder
McMahon & Gray, contractors
McKenna, Wm., butter merchant
Storey, Mrs., eating house

Local Residents

John Madden esq., D.L., Hilton Park
John Cole esq., Clontivern
Joseph Carson, esq., J.P. Cloncorn
Henry Pringle, esq., Clonboy
Wm Park, esq., J.P. Clonboy
A. Crawford, Clonkirk Cottage
Marshall Fitzgerald, Clonavilla
A. Dudgeon, solicitor, Stirling Lodge
The Misses Hoskins, Alterate
Rev. Joseph Abbott, Diocesan curate
James A. Knight, Corkimmons
T. Bamford, Lisnaroe
James Pritchard, Ballyhoebridge
Robert Bamford, Ballyhoe
Samuel K. Jackson, Cara
Francis Lough, Legnakelly
R. M. Sullivan, esq., J.P., Summerhill
Rev. A.N. Haire Foster, Ballynure
Rev. Robert Kennedy, Ballyhoe
Mrs. Thompson, Glenvar, Cara

Belturbet Directory

The Diamond

Burnett, William, draper
Farley – publican
Fitzpatrick, John, butcher
Gillick, Walter, grocery and hardware
Leonard Brothers, drapers
Morrow, William, printer
Maghorn, Mrs., Temperance Hotel
Reburn, George, grocer & publican

Butler Street

Cockings, Charles, grocer & publican
Fitzpatrick, Peter, publican
Johnston, J. W., J. P., general merchant
Johnston, George, draper
Mahaffy, James, J. P. postmaster
Maxwell, Thomas, draper & grocer
McCardle, Edward, car owner
McClean, James, publican
Murphy – Royal Hotel
Richmond, George, grocer
Strain & Thompson, grocers, &c.
Walker, Robt., manager. Ulster Bank

Belturbet

Holburn Hill

Brady, Rev. John, P. P., V.C.
Conlay, - grocer & publican
Donaldson, Thomas, tailor

Lunn, John, marine dealer
Magowen, Robert, Medical Hall
Reilly, Thomas, whitesmith
Reilly, Robert, boot & shoemaker
Sheil, John, grocer & publican
Smith, Charles, grocer & publican
Baker, J., spirit-grocer, Barrack Hill

The Lawn

Annesley, S. T. St. J., surgeon
Black, Rev. J., Presbyterian Church
Fitzpatrick, J., coachbuilder
Gilsenan, Thomas, solicitor
Martin, Albert, butter merchant
Martin, Mrs., Commercial Hotel
Smith, Rev. P., curate, R. C. Church
Seroghan, J., dispensary doctor

Upper Bridge Street

Boland, Timothy, spirit-grocer
Bohill, T. P., draper
Bogue, James, publican
Dolan, Thomas, leather merchant
Fitzpatrick, John, publican
Follis, James, publican
Kennedy, Philip, spirit-grocer
McMahon, Mrs., publican
McQuaid, Miss, news-agent
Small, John, victualler
Sullivan, James, cooper
Vessey, Miss, publican

Lower Bridge Street

Breslan, Wm., watchmaker
Deering, Miss, spirit-grocer
Flood, John, grocer & baker
McAllister, John, carpenter
Reilly, Bernard, saddler
Sewell, James, cattle doctor
Storey, Miss, dressmaker & draper

Kilcunny

Berry, Thomas, C.P.S., Riverside
Bullock, Wm., auctioneer, Aghalane
Elliot, Rev. Alex., Methodist Manse
Heslin, John, spirit-grocer
Jermyn, F., cooper
Maynes, Thomas, carpenter
McLean, Wm, builder
Morton, Henry, mineral water maker
McDougal, Rev. Wm., parish church
Reilly, J., spirit-grocer
Shannon, Rev. John, C.C., Staghall
Yaw, John, J.P., spirit-grocer

Jackson, Rev. J. McC., The Rectory
Johnston, Wm., stationmaster
Lanesborough, Earl, Quivey Lodge
Leech, Rev. Robt., Drumlane Rectry.
Saunderson, Col., M.P., Castle Sndr.
Saunderson, Samuel, D.L.Cloverhill
Vernon, Fane, D.L., Erne Hill

Lisnaskea Town

Parish Church – Rev. W. C. Ledger, rector
Methodist Church – Rev. W. E. Lawson
R. C. Chapel – Rev. Canon Megan, P.P.
R.I.C. – G.E.Dagg, D.I., Derryrea;
Patrick Keenehan, Head Const.;
Samuel Murtagh, Sergeant ;
Peter Rudden, sergeant &
Insp.Weights & Measures;
Geo Clarke, acting sergt;
Constables Thos Algeo, John Cullen,
Robert Gillespie, John Maguire,
Jas Jennings, Michael McNaughton

Annon, Charles, victualler
Armstrong, Wm., grocer's assistant
Arnold, George, draper
Adams, Thomas, publican
Beresford, Thomas, engrocer
Berney, Miss, dressmaker
Bradshaw, R.&J., merchants
Bryson, John, merchant
Boland, Mrs. grocer
Browne, Mrs. grocer
Braydon, Mrs., grocer
Cassidy, Philip, publican
Conway, Patrick, blacksmith
Conlay, James, publican
Dunne, John, publican
Dunne, Arthur, hardware
Doonan, Matthew, spirit-grocer
Devers, Wm., clothier
Fleming, W.W. mangr.Ulster Bank
Fausett, Alexander, saddler
Fairburn, Wm., jeweller
Fausett, Mrs., draper
Forster Brothers, grocers
Gamble, James, stationmaster [?]
Graham, Miss, dealer
Gavan, Thomas, draper
Gavan, Patrick, publican
Huggard, Wm., clerk petty sessions
Haire, Jas. ex-clerk petty sessions
Hoey, J.O'R, clerk Lisnaskea Union
Howell, Mrs. boot shop
Irwin, Thomas, general merchant
Irwin, the Misses
Irvine, Christopher, baker
Keating, Samuel, grocer's assistant
Keirans, Miss, boot warehouse
Knox, Doctor Thomas
Large, Digby, general merchant
Lewis, Norman, land clerk
Maguire, John, draper
Maguire, Thos., grocer and publican
Maguire, Mrs., confectioner
Maguire, Miss, bookseller, newsagent
Magovern, Anthony, publican

Masterson, Mrs., and the Misses
Masterson, Samuel, general merchant
Morton, Miss, grocer
Mone, Charles, cattle dealer
Murphy, Wm., cooper
McClintock, Mrs., hardware
McCoy, David, cooper
McEnulty, Mrs., grocer
McCaffrey, Francis, railway porter
McManus, Frank, publican
McDonald, Patrick, Mail car owner
McCalden, David, draper
Nixon, Robert George, auctioneer
Nixon, Miss H. classical teacher
Neeson, John, fowl merchant
Noble, Archie., mercht. & hotel keeper
Phair, James, baker
Peel, John, railway gate keeper
Richardson, Wm., auctioneer
Ross, Miss, teacher Infant School
Reilly, John, railway signal man
Robinson, J. H. watchmaker
Robinson Brothers, boot makers
Robinson, Thomas, postmaster
Robinson, Misses, delph & fancy gds.
Thompson, Liddle, spirit grocer
Thompson, Mrs Regist. Druggist
Thompson, - victualler
Wilson, J. H., mercht.& hotel keeper
Winters, James, railway porter

Lisnaskea – Local Farmers, &c.

Archdall, Mrs., Clifton Lodge
Armstrong, Charles Drumguiff
Butler, Hon., Mrs Cavendish, Inisrath
Bussell, Mrs., Ballindaragh
Bryans, Alexander, Mullaghboy
Bryans, Wm., Derryadd
Cassidy, Francis, Manorwaterhouse
Charters, Wm., P.L.G.
Clerkin, J., blacksmith, Drumcaw
Cosgrove, John, grocer, Killard
Cosgrove, Bernard, shoemaker, Killard
Collins, Jeremiah, Derryanny
Collins, John, Derryadd
Costello, J.F. Manorwaterhouse N.S.
Connolly, J. Gortgranagh
Crawford, John,P.L.G. Derryadd
Clingan, James, Derrylee
Dickson, Miss, Hollybrooke
Downey, James, Kilturk N.
Ebbit, James, Farnaconaghy
Fawcett, J. Derryadd
Forster, J. Cormonlea
Fawcett, Wm., Derrylee
Forster, Mrs., Lisagurry
Flanagan, E. M., P.L.G.
Fleming, Archibald, Killard
Fyffe, Thomas, Shanaghy
Gardiner, Edward, J.P. Gortgranagh
Gardiner, Mrs., Coragh
Gardiner, James, Drumlone
Gardiner, S., Dernish
Graham, Christopher, Derrylea
Hanna, George, Tirraffy
Hanna, Wm., Drumbrughas
Kettyle, Mrs, Derryadd
Kelly, John, Cornshea
Kelly, Robert, ex-sergt., 27th Regt
Kerr, W. J. roadmaker, Maughley
Ledger, Rev. W. C. rectory, Attybarn
Liddle, George, roadmaker, Derrylee
Little, Robert, Cushwash mills
Logan, John, Branish
Maguire, Philip, Mullaghboy
Maguire, Thomas, J.P., Munville
Maguire, John, cattle dealr. Munville
Maguire, Mrs., Carrick House
Maguire, Hugh, cattle dealr. Baltreagh
Maguire, Jas., teacher, Drumlone School
Maguire, John, Aghamore
Maguire, James, Derrylea
Marshall, Wm., Drumcrew
Maze, Matthew, Derrycannon
Maze, Mrs., Derrycannon
Megan, Rev, Canon, P.P.

Morrison, George, Cornashea
Morrison, John, Manorwaterhouse
Muldoon, Michael, Derrylea
Mulligan, James, Baltreagh
Murphy, John, grocer, Drumhose
McClelland, Samuel, Cormonlea
McConnel, Hugh, teacher, No.1 N.S.
McCormack, James, Mullaghboy
McCusker, John, Corsale
McDonagh, Thomas, Baltreagh
McDonald, John, Sallaghy
McIlwaine, John, Drumcaw
McMahon, Patr., teacher, No.2 N.S.
McManus, James, Tattygar
Noble, Archibald, Glassdrummond
Noble, William, Drumcunny
Noble, Archey, rate coll., Drumcunny
Patterson, J., Castlebalfour
Plunkett, Ralph, Derryadd
Plunkett, Jeremiah, Derryadd
Plunkett, Thomas, Derryadd
Robinson, Miss, Drumhose
Scholes, Andrew, P.L.G.
Sheil, Doctor, Mountcharles
Sherry, George, Ports
Sherry, Alexander, Cullindoo
Scott, Ben, road maker, Cornavrey
Tisdall, H.M., Manorwaterhouse
Thompson, Miss., Croghan
Tarlton, Wm., Clinmin
Winslow, B.T., solicitor, Forfey
Woods, John, Tullynevan
Woods, Alexander, Tullynevan
Waterson, Rev. Jas., Sallaghy, Glebe

Brookborough – Town & Vicinity

Armstrong, Wm., leather merchant
Armstrong, Sarah, publican
Brooke, Sir Arthur Douglas, D.L., J.P.
Baker, Eliza, draper   [Colebrooke
Bloomfield, John jun., draper
Bloomfield, John sen., carpenter
Bryson, Wm., merchant

Beatty, James, J.P. Killartry
Beatty, John A., R.O., Killykeiran
Bogue, Thomas, Stonepark
Cassidy, James, publican
Clinton, Rev. John, Aghavey Rectory
Coulter, Samuel, merchant
Doran, Colonel, Lurganbrae
Dalton, Thomas, P.L.G., Littlemount
Dickson, Robert, constable, R.I.C.
Doonan, Alexander, victualler
Doonan, James, Liscosker
Dunn, John, farmer
Funston, Richard, postmaster
Gilkinson, Thomas, stationmaster
Gillespie, John, carpenter
Johnston, James F., merchant
Jordan, James, farmer, Drummee
Jordan, John, farmer, Tatnavar
Kenny, John, ex-constable, R.I.C
Kane, Joseph, tailor
Kelly, Thomas, dealer, Mowens Cross
Law, Margaret, teacher, No.2. N.S.
Lendrum, Robert, sculptor
McKenna, Rev. Canon, P.P., Tullynagowan
McMeel, Rev. P., C.C.
McBarron, Patrick, teacher, No.1 N.S.
McDowell, Samuel, saddler
McCutcheon, Wm., sergeant, R.I.C.
McCardle, James, publican
McConnell, John, C.P.S. & land agent
McGoldrick, James, ex-constable
McHugh, John, constable, R.I.C.
Moore, Rev. Hugh, Methodist Manse
Mears, Andrew, Ballyreagh
Murphy, Samuel, A., merchant
Owens, James, ex-schoolteacher
Patton, J.G., teacher, Littlemount N.S.
Roulstone, Wm., blacksmith
Rea, Thompson, Tullynagowan
Reide, Nicholas, constable R.I.C.
Smith, John A., Skeog
Taylor, esq., T.C., medical officer
West, Captain A.G., Whitepark

Donagh – Directory to Locality

Bryans, Wm., farmer, Moorlough
Collins, Thomas, farmer, Donagh
Crudden, Thomas, farmer, Lettergreen
Davis, James, scutcher, Donagh
Irwin, Andrew, road maker, Tattygar
Maguire, John, farmer, Rockfield
Morrow, T., post office, publican, &c.
Moore, John, farmer, Moorlough
Mowen, Pat, farmer, Killmacbrack
Mowen, Pat, farmer, Lettergreen
Murray, Alex., grocer & road maker
McDonald, B. roadmaker, Lettergreen.
McDermott, James, scutcher, Donagh
McDonald, Wm., roadmaker, Tattygar
McManas, Jas., scutcher, Drumgallon
McMahon, James, farmer, Rockfield
McManas, Francis, frmr., Moorlough
McRoe, Misses, tchrs. Donagh N.S.
Parker, esq., Robert, Fairview House
Rooney, James, miller, Donagh
Skelton, esq., Francis, Donagh House
Shields, Edward, scutcher, Donagh
Swift, Philip, farmer, Donagh
Watson, Thomas, farmer, Donagh

Magheraveely – Principal Inhabitants

Clarke, J., Postmaster
Clendinning, John, grocer
Collins, Patrick, publican
Clarke, Miss, dressmaker
McCutcheon, Edward, sexton
Howe, Thos, grocer
Morrison, John, grocer
Wiggins, Wm, ex-const. R.I.C.

Directory to the Locality

Armstrong, Mrs., Clincarn
Armstrong, Thomas, Drumma
Armstrong, John, Drimmusky
Armstrong, Samuel, Keiranbeg
Beggan, Thomas, Coolnasilla
Brady, Wm., esq., Johnstown
Clarke, John, Midhill
Clarke, Miss, M, teacher, Midhill, N.S.
Coulson, Samuel, Belmount
Edgerton, Joseph, Derraghree
Edgerton, Thomas, Clonfeil
Elliott, James, Drumbinisk
Haire, Major W.H., Armagh-manor
Hutchinson, Samuel, Agharooskey E.
Hutchinson, Robert, Conkera
Johnston, Wm., Coolnamarrow
Johnston Joseph, Tully
Johnston, Mrs., Lisnamallard
King, Alexander, Lisnamallard
Lynch, James, blacksmith, Clonfail
Maguire, Hugh, J.P. Tully
Mayne, Samuel, Rateen
Mayne, John, Golan
Nixon, John, Clonatty
Phillips, J., esq., Magheramore
Quinn. Hugh, teacher, Rateen N.S.
Rawlins, T.R., esq., Scotsboro'
Richardson, esq., Robt., Summerhill
Rennick, Arthur, Maghereagh
Rutledge, David, P.L.G., Ratoal
Stack, Rt., Rev., Charles M., Bishop
    of Clogher, Knockballymore
Sullivan, Rev. G.B. Aghadrumsea
Tierney, John, Rathmoran
West, James, Drummuskey
Wiggins, Wm. H., Rate coll., Knox
Wilson, Robert, Whitehill
Wilson, J., Gowney

Newtownbutler -Town

Galloon Par.Ch. – Rev. G.G. Parkinson-Cumine, M.A. Rectory
Methodist Church –Rev. A.M. Rutledge
R.C.Church – Revs. Canon O'Connor & H. O'Neil, C.C., the presbytery.

James Bell, farmer, The Cottage
Thomas, Kenny, constable, R.I.C.
Mrs Johnston
H. Robinson, P.C.M. Missionary
Hugh Keating, constable, R.I.C.
Miss Graydon. Miss Moore
John Murray, sergeant, R.I.C.
William Logan, constable, R.I.C.
Miss Cosgrove, dressmaker
Christopher Bellew, Insur. Agent
James McBride, constable, R.I.C.
Miss Ketty Smith. Miss B. Harpur
Miss Sarah Clarke, ex-postmistress
Thomas Beatty, victualler & farmer
James Courtney, post office
Henry Courtney, Postmaster
Samuel A. Clugston, schoolmaster
Alexander Keating, grocer
Wm. Nixon, commercial traveller
James Maguire, builder, &c.
Michael Clerkin, shoemaker
Miss Clerkin, milliner
John Maguire, merchant
Patrick Maguire, farmer
James Cooke, clerk of Petty Sessions
Saml. Clarke, esq., farmer
The Misses Peters, farmers
Miss Watson, propr. Watson's Forge
Miss Kelly, egg dealer
Pat McDermott, labourer
Mrs Reilly, spirit-grocer, the hotel
John Reilly, grocer and news agent
Philip Reilly, esq., J.P. farmer
Thomas Duffy, grocer
Dennis McCaffrey, grocer
Hugh McDonald, shoemaker
James McKeeve, grocer
John McGinn, baker
John Swift, blacksmith
Robert Maguire, grocer and druggist, -Printer of Newtownbutler Herald
Samuel Holt, railway overseer
Patrick Meehan, plasterer
Hugh Bell, sexton of parish church
Mrs Maguire, Temperance Hotel prop.
Dr. Barrington
Thomas Irwin, creamery manager
James Hamilton, farmer
Wm. Elliott, railway labourer
Mrs Hand, railway gate keeper
John Taggart, constable R.I.C.
John Johnston, esq., J.P. merchant
Mrs Campbell
Thomas Lang, grocery manager
Andrew Knox, J. Edgerton, grocers
James Lang, draper
James Beatty, horse trainer
Tom Wilson, fowl dealer
Dr. Francis Crighton Fitzgerald
Dr. James Fitzgerald
The Misses Fitzgerald
James Fitzgerald, Deputy Registrar
Henry Barton, railway carpenter
Samuel R. Molloy, constable, R.I.C.
John Corrigan, summons server
Thomas Hand, carpenter
Mrs Lang, farmer, Milltown
John Dogherty, stationmaster
Mrs Dogherty, schoolmistress
Mrs Jane Thompson, grocer
James Greenan, baker
M. Reilly & Son, merchant tailors
Margt. Gunn, lodging-house keeper
Richard Clifford, dealer
John Sheridan, tailor
Miss Johnston, dressmaker
John Nicholl, shoemaker
Wm. Sherry, lodging-house keeper
Daniel McElroy, Shoemaker
Misses Hicks, dressmakers

Mrs Ellen Mowen, spirit-grocer
Wm. Lawrence

Newtownbutler – Country Farmers, &c.

Allen, Robert, Clinaroo
Allen, Thomas, Mullaghgar
Allen, Mrs., Farm
Allen, Richard, Aughnahinch
Allen, Wm., Legmacaffrey
Allen, Robert, Legmacaffrey
Armstrong, Ed., carpenter, Lislaris
Armstrong, George, Killycornan
Armstrong, Frank, Lisnaknock
Bailey, Alexander, Killycornan
Beggins, Edward, Clinaroo
Beatty, Wm., Derrydoon
Browne, A.H. Lurganboy
Browne, Wm., Gortbrannon
Brookes, Wm., Aughnahinch
Bussell, John, Corsinchin House
Bussell, Mrs, Garrorooskey
Carey, John, Killespenan
Conlan, Frank, Landbrock
Courtney, John, mason, Kilgarrow
Crozier, John G., esq., Gortra House
Coulter, Thos., Legmacaffrey
Crudden, John, J.P. Carrigans
Clindining, Ed., Killycornan
Dogherty, Jas., teacher, No.2. N.S.
Donegan, John, Corlatt
Doogan, Thomas, Drumrain
Doonan, John, Un. Insp., Kilroot
Dawson, James, Mullabredin
Edgerton, John, Ballywilliam
Elliott, James, Mullnagoan
Fawcett, John James, Kilnacran
Forster, Charles, Artinagh
Fitzpatrick, James, Derrykenny
Flemming, Hugh, P.L.G. Bunn
Flemming, Henry, Derrycorby
Gilroy, James, Leitrim

Goodfrey, James, Clinaroo
Gould, William, Cornabrass
Gray, John Robert, Derryelvin
Graydon, Wm., Pipershill
Gunn, Pat, carpenter, Bohora
Hicks, Wm., Bunn
Hetherington, John, Cullion
Irwin, [blank] Derrybeg
Jones, John, Cullion
Johnston, Thomas, Doohatt
Jones, Andy, Cullion
Little, Andrew, Leitrim
Little, John, Leitrim
Liddle, Mrs, Killalahard
Liddle, Robert, Kilturk
Liddle, Joseph, Killalahard
Maguire, Hugh, Aughnahinch
Maguire, Jas., cooper, Derryginnedy
McClure, John, cattle dlr., Derrycorby
Moore, John, music teacher, Clinkee
Mowen, Patrick, Lettergreen
Morton, Edward, Killalahard
Moore, Saml. cess coll. Lisnashellidy
Moore, Alexander, Sheeney
McCusker, Jas., brick mkr. Cornavrey
McClosky, Miss, tchr. Derryginnedy N.S.
McKernan, Jas. N. Isp. Drumbrughas
Neil, James, Corasaul
Nixon, R., pros.srvr., Derryginnedy
Nixon, R. shopkeeper, Derrycorby
O'Neil, J. teacher, Wattlebridge N.S.
Parkinson, James, Cornabrass
Robinson, Wm., Feaugh N.S.
Scarlett, John, Lislaris
Scott, John, Cornavrey
Thompson, Samuel, Cornabrass
Thompson, Isaac, Cornabrass
Taggart, Doctor, Manorhighgate
Tierney, James, J.P. Drumrain
Thompson, Wm., teacher, Feaugh
Wadsworth, Wm. H. Drumcrew
Wadsworth, James, Drumralla

Wadsworth, James, Gortion
Welsh, Mrs., Drumbrughas
West, T.W., Mullyduff
West, James, Clinelty
West, Wm., Drumralla
West, John, Kilgarrow
West, Frank, Knockmakiggan
Williams, Miss, tchr. Killalahard N.S
Williams, Joseph, Mullnahorn

Maguiresbridge – Town & Vicinity

Parish Church – Rev. A.A. Watson M.A.
Methodist Ch. – Rev. John J. Hutchinson
Presbyterian Ch. – Rev. Robert Boyle
R.C. Chapel – Rev. P. McCleery
Schools: No.1 – W.G. Irvine, teacher
No.2 – Wm. Moore, teacher
R.I.C. – Sergt. Coulter, Constables
Heslin, Murphy, Kiernan and Murray

Aiken, Acheson, medical doctor
Charters, Thomas, grocer &c
Connolly, Thomas, boot & shoemaker
Crawford, Hy. Tullynorth mills
Delmore, William, shoemaker
Ferris, John, blacksmith
Gormerly, John, fowl merchant
Graham, F J, D.L., J.P., Drumgoon
Graham, Mrs John, dressmaker
Graham, Wm. grocer
Henderson, esq., W.G.
Haslett, Wm., miller, Boyhill
Hamilton, Robt., postmaster, grocer
Hamilton, Isaac, Lonsdale Hotel
Howe, Robert, blacksmith
Irvine, William Henry
Knight, L P. [high]sheriff, Abbeylodge
Little, M [blank]& delph-ware
[indecipherable], draper & grocer
[Lynch?], Michael, hardware & spirits
Lynch, Mary, grocery & spirits
Matthews, Geo., Hollymount House
Morrison, Miss Mary, dressmaker

Maguire, Robrt. ex-sergt. R.I.C.
Martin, Thomas, farmer
Mulligan, John, farmer & carpenter
McAloon, S. spirit mercht. & farmer
McAvinney, James, shoemaker
McCaddam, Patrick, egg merchant
McCullough, Wm., general merchant

St. Mary's Church, Maguiresbridge

McManus, Patrick, merchant tailor
McCarthy, Callaghan, ex-const. R.I.C.
McGovern, Peter, draper
McGowan, Robert, stationmaster
Murphy, esq., J.P. James, Drumliff
Mulligan, esq. J.P. James, Droles
Naan, Francis, baker & grocer
O'Harra, Thomas, farmer
Parkinson, David, grocer
Porteous, the Misses
Rutledge, Richard, Railway Cottage
Ruddel, Wm., PCM missionary
Reynolds, Wm., farmer
Simpson, James, ex-const. & bailiff
Wiley, Mrs, miller, Drumgoon
Welsh, Henry, sheriff's bailiff

Rose McCaughey 1925-2010

Rose McCaughey (nee McAuley) who died 25 October 2010 aged 85 was a founding member of the Fermanagh Authors' Association and a popular member of staff in Enniskillen Library for many years.

Rose, who was born in New York, had many stories about living in the Bronx during the era of the Wall Street Crash.

'...as a child I can remember watching the long queues of men and women queuing for food. My mother explained to me that these people had lost their jobs and had no money to buy food or clothes. So the government sponsored kitchens were their only means of keeping body and soul together and many men slept in doorways and spent their daylight hours seeking any kind of work such as sweeping snow off the streets in winter. A number of emigrants who had a bit of money saved returned to their country of origin. However the banks after some time only paid out investors 25% of their savings. I remember an elderly couple who lived in the apartment next to ours having to leave for a much cheaper rent flat in Upper Manhattan. I still can remember them crying as they were saying goodbye to their neighbours.

She also had vivid memories of first seeing Enniskillen at the age of nine when her family moved back to Ireland, her parents being natives of the Dowra area of County Cavan. They stayed for a few days in the Railway Hotel where in the 1930s there were no en suite bedrooms, just one bathroom at the end of the corridor. Unable to get a house in town the McAuleys bought a farm at Mullylogan, now on the outskirts of Enniskillen. Rose attended the local convent schools and was surprised that the nuns used corporal punishment as the sisters in New York did not. She also remembered children from the workhouse attending school in their workhouse uniforms.

Rose married Paddy McCaughey in 1949, they had seven children, and celebrated their 50th wedding anniversary in 2009 several months before Paddy's death.

Rose worked for the library service from 1974-1990 in the special services division, providing books and audio materials to the hospitals and the housebound. This was an ideal position for her as she was very interested in people and loved books. After she retired Rose, who was a very sociable person, was involved in many local groups including the U3A (University of the Third Age) and Fermanagh Talking Newspaper and remained active until her final illness.

Rose was proud of her American birth and always exercised her right to vote in American presidential elections.

She was also a popular member of the writers' group which met in the Clinton Centre and wrote many articles and short stories, some of which were published in *The Spark* and the *Fermanagh Miscellany*.

Johnny McKeagney 1938-2010

Johnny McKeagney, local historian and artist died suddenly 1 December 2010, just five weeks after the publication of *In the Auld Ago,* his monumental collection of illustrated folklore and townland profiles.

Johnny, who was born into a family of craftsmen, was village shopkeeper and undertaker in Tempo for many years. A largely self-taught artist he specialised in drawing old houses and monuments, farm implements and wildlife. Not content simply to draw what he saw, he also talked to people in the locality and used their memories to enhance his pictures. Thus he was able to recreate old derelict buildings and imagine them as they once had been: the corn mill, the creamery as centres of activity, or the hearth, focus of the family that gathered around it.

Johnny loved to walk an area and meet the local people, to get the feel of a place, the lie of the land. He understood the importance of recording what he saw and heard and so, although the drawing pen was his chosen medium of expression, he also used the tape recorder and camera to great effect to chronicle what he found. And so his drawings and the text that accompanied them are multi-dimensional, presenting an interweave of folklore, local history and personal perspective in a unique way.

It would be no exaggeration to say that Johnny was addicted to his research. He delighted in meeting people and hearing their stories. He loved to open up a new area and in the months before his death he had been spending a lot of time in north west Cavan.

He also had a special interest in old graveyards, recognising them as places full of history and memories. He appreciated the craft of the stone mason and took great care, not just to transcribe inscriptions, but to draw every stone and copy the lettering and carvings. Of particular interest were the graveyards of Pubble near Tempo, and those on Devenish island. Johnny spent many days in both of these locations discovering stones not previously recorded, and succeeded in deciphering inscriptions which had baffled previous researchers.

Although Johnny was widely respected and acknowledged as a man of great knowledge and talent, many feared that his work might never be made available in a format that would preserve it and make it accessible to all. So it was a great relief to family and friends when Johnny's book was published last year. And having once taken the plunge Johnny was already talking about the next book. Sadly Johnny did not live to enjoy all the acclaim that his book must have brought him but he has left a huge body of work, an archive forty years in the making, published and unpublished, which will prove an invaluable source in years to come.

T P Flanagan Remembered
by Michael Donnelly

Terry - T. P. Flanagan - was born in Enniskillen in 1929, the eldest of seven children of William and Margaret (nee Maguire), a local couple. Margaret died in 1935 and William left for Dublin leaving Terry and his sisters Julia and Joan in the care of his sisters, who lived above Lipton's shop in the Hollow. They spent formative holidays with another aunt, Elizabeth, who was involved with the Gore Booth family of Lissadel House, Sligo.

Terry progressed from the primary school run by Presentation Brothers to the secondary school nearby. The principal Bro. Bede was a qualified art teacher and Terry's talent in this and English was quickly recognized. However, art was not a core subject for Senior Certificate examination, and Terry attended evening classes under Kathleen Bridle at the Tech. She was a practicing artist in watercolour who had also taught the noted artist and woodcarver, William Scott. Terry performed with distinction in schools drama at the local festival and took top place in English in his Senior Leaving Cert. However, a weak maths result caused him to repeat it for entry to his chosen course and he succeeded, also repeating his English achievement.

He attended the College of Art in Belfast where he again came in contact with a noted watercolourist, W. Penrose. He also formed lifelong friendships, including Basil Blackshaw, an artist not dissimilar in style and approach. On qualifying he taught initially in girls grammar schools before taking up a long career in St. Mary's training college for teachers.

After our school days, I next met him on the road near Bawnboy when I was returning from graduation. He was in a horse drawn caravan and wore bohemian garb and a large knife in his belt, not exactly like the rather detached boy of schooldays. Later I attended life classes in the College of Art where he and Basil shared the work with John Luke. His approach to tutoring was less magisterial than theirs and one of the other students was Sheelagh Garvin, an actress with the Lyric Theatre, whom he married in August 1959. I was in the church and the bride was rather late, arriving just as Terry's anxiety was beginning to show. I met him infrequently thereafter, mostly on occasions where we had a common interest. I purchased four of his works, two each for myself and Theresa. In reference to one, Cloonabawn, he told my wife, Theresa that it represented not a particular place or subject but rather his take on the many derelict dwellings in the picture area. It was a title system he frequently employed.

While he was always his own man following a very individual path, he had a catholic appreciation of other artists work, very different to his own. He could articulate it in concise and authoritative fashion. I remember his panegyric at the funeral of William Scott. As an architect I appreciated his virtuosity both in draughtmanship and his control of a very difficult medium, particularly in large pictures. His compositions emerged as a realization of a concept, unlike many now where the work develops a germ of an idea, during execution. They are faithful to form, yet economical and spare almost to abstract and they have the architectural qualities of repose and dynamic tension. He became a revered local as well as a national icon and a charismatic character. "Go ndéana Dia trócaire ar a anam uasal" (May God have mercy on his noble soul.)

T. P. Flanagan

An Academician of the Royal Hibernian Academy and a past president of the Royal Ulster Academy. He celebrated his 80th birthday in 2010, the same year he received an honorary doctorate in fine art from the University of Ulster.

T. P. Flanagan Remembered

by Dermot Maguire

In the 1960's when I was attending St. Joseph's Training College (Trench House) on the Stewartstown Road in West Belfast we were sent down the Falls Road to St. Mary's Training College for painting classes with Terence Flanagan. There was a rumour that he was a Fermanagh man. On our first visit to him, I have to admit, my greenhorn eyes and ears neither saw nor heard much that was characteristically Fermanagh about Terence P. Flanagan. His manner was somewhat otherworldly, but his talk and teaching was always encouraging and it was obvious in no time at all that this was a man 'into his subject.' Very soon too, we all (I think) got to appreciate his great mastery of language. We knew instinctively that he was an artist in thought, word and deed - the genuine article. If he was a bit 'other,' that was because he was 'a rale artist.' Soon, the fact that he was a Fermanagh man seemed irrelevant.

During that momentous college year of 1968-69 when Civil Rights marches and street politics were often in the frame more than lectures, it seems to me now that Flanagan's classes were an oasis of calm. A sense of stillness within the man is what I took away with me after that year. Many years later I remember going to hear him give a talk in the Ulster Museum. There again was the flow of language and the deep engagement with the subject. A friend, who had never heard Flanagan speak, said he could have listened to him all day and that he never thought a painter could speak like that - painters were expected to speak through their work not their mouths, but Terry Flanagan could do both.

Flanagan once said that he could not go to Connemara without seeing the Twelve Pins the way Paul Henry saw them. In the same way, I now see Fermanagh and Lough Erne in particular, through T. P. Flanagan's vision. Besides all his great technical skills - of composition, structure and drawing, and his achievements in watercolour, Flanagan's work for me is infused with that same stillness and self-assurance that I remember in the man all those years ago. The man and the artist were pretty well inseparable and that, of course, is the reason why his work has soul and will surely last.

T. P. Flanagan with his wife Sheelagh.
He died on 22nd February 2011 aged 80 years

I suppose, now that he is dead, it is not irrelevant (if it ever was) that he was a Fermanagh man - we will always want to claim him.

Ar ais go Keriolet- Back to Keriolet by Seamas Mac Annaidh

Reviewed by Michael Donnelly

The latest novel by Seamus Mac Annaidh is, as always, in Gaelic, and as always, demonstrates a quirky individualism of subject and treatment. The subject matter is well served in writing in English and this may be the first to treat of it in the language of a challenged and not to say, hostile indigenous culture. That is a challenge the book faces, and as it fits none of the genre boxes, cannot be assessed in accordance with these.

The story starts pre-World War I, centred on George Burdell, sole surviving scion of Lantytown House, the family suffering status decline from social change, revolution and the usual primogeniture problems. Everything is told almost autobiographically and in colloquial exchange. We meet him firstt as a child in the world of his mother's family, a world of single women and no siblings or young relatives. They communicate to him a strong sense of family but no joined up story. He is, then, lonely but well endowed, financially, and with an unfulfilled sense of identity. He grows up, schooled in the traditional life of the Anglo Pale, an area where the author is sure footed and convincing generally. He, George, has an abiding interest in recovering and perhaps, recreating the lost and perhaps, distinguished past. He encounters some devious elements in this quest and the hazards of collecting are well conveyed. He is diverted to Brittany to look at a possible and available alternative to Lantytown House, and now the story becomes historic novel in mode, dealing with an actual place and its aristocratic Russian emigre owner, Prince Youssoupoff. His prospective client receives from him, in speech and writing, the whole tale of the Romanoffs and Rasputin of whom he himself was the principal assassin. The account is told with some fashionable shiver but well short of horror movie mode. The written story reveals an authorial empathy with the lost culture of the Orthodox Church and its world. In Brittany he also encounters with a degree of detachment again, the ambivalent aspects of French and Breton relationships, and which parallels something of his Irish experience.

The Breton venture is somewhat unconvincingly terminated and back in Ireland we have a fast forward switch to 1990s Ireland dealing with George's marriage, career, family life and widowhood in a short paragraph. George emerges older, perhaps wiser but still obsessed with the unfulfilled dream. His partial realization of this through his family and the final twists and turns demonstrate the author's interest in and his distrust of folk history and the possible moral of message lies in this. George's failure to receive or communicate to his own offspring any sense of the relevance of the past to the present and maybe, in the author's view that is all to the good also.

The personnel are cast like actors in a play, their characters affecting events but remaining unchanged. Also, as in a play script much of the story is conveyed in direct speech. People are described only to the extent the part requires. Buildings are described almost anatomically without emotional response which is in character with the story. The language is not in its cultural comfort zone and lacks colour but it is a story requiring detachment and opening the language to different worlds and themes. The twists and turns of the plot have murder mystery character but, perhaps, in the case of the train incident open to question. The blurb would lead us to expect an updated Rex Carlo story, however, Seamus is not about reproducing popular genre in Gaelic but in the ability of writing in Irish to command its own literary domain. Go n'eiri an t'adh leis an obair.

Fermanagh publications 2010

*denotes member of Fermanagh Authors' Association

Alison Brown
Bible Numbers EDINBURGH: Banner of Truth ISBN 1848710275.

*John Cunningham and *Dianne Trimble
Fermanagh Miscellany 2010 ENNISKILLEN: Fermanagh Authors' Association ISBN 978 1 907530 15 9. 114 pages softback.

Mary Gordon
Enniskillen in the Rare Ould Times II ENNISKILLEN: Millennium Babes 181 pages, softback.

Ederney Festival Committee
A quilt and book *"Townlands of the Glendarragh Valley"* 34 pages.

*Vicky Herbert
Lisnaskea Workhouse: Past, Present and Hopefully Future Davog Press ISBN 978-1-907530-01-2   54 pages, A5 softback.

Mary Valerie Irwin
Four West Clogher Churches: A History, Cluff Printing Services, 138 pgs, A5 paperback.

Killyhommon Primary School
Inspirational Diary 2011 (published 2010) softback

Mary Lynch
The Long Road Home Londubh Books ISBN 9781907535086. 256 pages, softback.

Johnny McKeagney
In The Auld Ago, illustrated Irish Folklore [the author] ISBN 978-0-9566976-0-8. 203 pages, hardback.

Moat Primary School and St. Ronan's Primary School
Book on Lisnaskea

Samuel Boyd Morrow
Farming in County Fermanagh. Development in the Twentieth Century. ISBN 978-0956699701 340 pages, hardback.

*John James Reihill
Friday's Child – 70 Years of Island Life [autobiography] 236 pages softback

Paddy Tyson
The Hunt for Puerto Del Faglioli: A motorcycle adventure in search of the improbable. Shuvvy Press ISBN 978-0956430502 395 pages, softback.

Bob Wilsdon
Plantation Castles on the Erne History Press ISBN 978 45889807. softback

Contributors

Ruthanne Baxter, originally from Pettigo, taught music in Fermanagh before moving to the mainland where she has worked for the Scottish Arts Council in South Ayrshire and is currently Arts Education Manager for East Lothian. She has recorded and broadcast her short stories on BBC Radio Ulster and her poetry has been included in anthologies by Dogma Publication, Oxford.

Anthony Brady has lived in Brockagh, Tempo since 1997. He is London born, originating in Co Tyrone, and he has lived in France and Belgium. He is formerly a Social Work/Housing Team Manager with Camden Council. His poems are published by Forward Press; his short story, *Sister of Mercy*, appeared in *Ireland's Own*.

John B. Cunningham is chairman of the Fermanagh Authors' Association and a retired schoolmaster, living in Belleek. He has written extensively on the local history of counties Fermanagh, Donegal, Cavan and Monaghan. His first book which appeared in 1980 has been followed by more than thirty more where he has been writer, editor or major contributor. Today he works as a genealogist and is a qualified Irish National Tour Guide. His most recent books are listed in the Fermanagh Publications section above.

Brian D'Arcy C.P. is the Rector of St Gabriel's Retreat, the Graan, Enniskillen. He is also a noted author, newspaper columnist and broadcaster. He presents the BBC radio programmes, *Sunday Half Hour* and *Sunday with Brian D'Arcy* and he has a regular residency on *Chris Evans Breakfast Show*. He has authored more than 10 books; his latest book is *A Little Bit of Healing*.

Michael Donnelly is a retired architect from Enniskillen. He published *The Fate of the Sons of Toirann* in 1999.

Bryan Gallagher is a retired headmaster who has spent his whole life living in the county of Fermanagh near the beautiful shores of Lough Erne. His first book, *There'll Not be a Crowd till the Crowd Gathers*, was a memoir of the Starlight Dance Band of which he was a member. His first collection of stories, *Barefoot in Mullyneeny*, was published by Harper Collins in 2005 and received outstanding reviews.

Winston Graydon was born in Brookeborough but has lived in Belfast for the past forty-five years. His memoir of Fermanagh in the 1940's, *The Oul County in Story and Verse*, was published in 2008. His story, *The Mountain Man (A Fermanagh Story)* was published in the spring, 2009.

Vicky Herbert has been a Heritage Tour Guide for 16 years at Crom National Trust Estate and in Lisnaskea. Always interested in local history and the people that made it, Vicky has produced three books on Crom, two on Lisnaskea and three of interviews with local characters. Her most recent book is *Lisnaskea Workhouse: Past, Present and Hopefully Future*.

Seamas Mac Annaidh has published fifteen books since 1982 when his first novel, *Cuaifeach Mo Lon Dubh Bui* appeared. He was writer-in-residence at Galway University for 2007-09 but retains his links with his home town of Enniskillen.

Sean McElgunn was born in Belturbet in 1930. He spent many years as a missionary priest in the Phillipines. Now married and living in Cashel, Belcoo he is the author of seven books, the most recent of which *World without Women* was published in September 2007.

Cahir McKeown was born in Enniskillen and educated at St. Michael's Primary School at the East Bridge and Enniskillen Technical College. A retired lecturer in building construction and painting at Fermanagh College he is the author of *Enniskillen Reminiscences: The Life and Times in Enniskillen, 1930s* (1993) and *1848 - 1998 150 years Blessed Virgin Conference St. Vincent de Paul Society* Enniskillen (2002).

Dermot Maguire is a retired teacher who taught in Belfast for over 30 years and is now living back in his home townland of Derrylea. Having spent the last 25 years collecting the folklore and history of his native place he published *Drumlone at the Crossroads* in 2005.

Frank McHugh was born to Fermanagh parents in 1963, and he works at Portora Royal School as Head of Drama. He set up the Fermanagh branch of the North of Ireland Family History Society in 2008 and he is Secretary of the branch.

Mary Montague grew up in Ederney, Co Fermanagh, and worked for many years as a biology teacher in Derry. Her first poetry collection, *Black Wolf on a White Plain*, was published by Summer Palace Press in 2001, and her second, *Tribe*, by Dedalus Press in 2008. Her work was anthologised most recently in *Four Irish Poets*, (Dedalus Press 2011; ed: Clíona Ní Ríordáin), a bilingual selection in English and French. She is currently studying for a PhD on bird song. She lives in Belfast and in Co Derry.

John Reihill was born on Inishcorkish island on Upper Lough Erne where he farmed and ran a successful restaurant business with his wife Sheila. Author of *Reflections of an Islander; Hands Across the Sea* which tells his mother's story and *Where's My Begonia, Rose?* he published *Friday's Child – 70 years of island life*, his autobiography in 2010.

Julie Richmond has lived in Fermanagh for more than a decade. A dancer from an early age, and dance teacher for 15 years, her interests are photography and performance art. She has been involved in social and community care for many years which inspired her digital art books, including *Life*, a devotional book published in 2007 and, more recently, *Go Beyond Reality* and *In The Life Of An Aerial*.

Dianne Trimble is a Canadian, living near Brookeborough. She writes in her spare time and her articles and stories have been printed in Canadian and Irish newspapers and magazines, including the *Toronto Star*, *Ireland's Own* and *Senior Times*. She is a member of the Brookeborough Historical Society and contributed material to their local history book, *The Brookeborough Story*. Her first novel, an historical fiction, *Hitler and Mars Bars*, was released under her maiden name, Dianne Ascroft in 2008.